the paths
of gracie

the paths

of gracie

kriston whitledge-knaust

TATE PUBLISHING & Enterprises

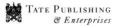

TATE PUBLISHING
& *Enterprises*

Tate Publishing is committed to excellence in the publishing industry. Our staff of highly trained professionals, including editors, graphic designers, and marketing personnel, work together to produce the very finest books available. The company reflects the philosophy established by the founders, based on Psalms 68:11,

"THE LORD GAVE THE WORD AND GREAT WAS THE COMPANY OF THOSE WHO PUBLISHED IT."

If you would like further information, please contact us:
1.888.361.9473 | www.tatepublishing.com
TATE PUBLISHING & *Enterprises*, LLC | 127 E. Trade Center Terrace
Mustang, Oklahoma 73064 USA

The Paths of Gracie

This novel is a work of fiction. Names, descriptions, entities and incidents included in the story are products of the author's imagination. Any resemblance to actual persons, events and entities is entirely coincidental.

Published in the United States of America

ISBN: 978-1-6024732-0-1

07.03.30

foreword

God created us for community and we need one another. Yet, there are times in our lives when it is not easy to fit in. *The Paths of Gracie* skillfully examines such a time in the life of eighth grader Gracie Williams. Nothing is happening in her life as Grace expected and being with the "popular" girls is a lot more work than she imagined. Grace must not only learn the eighth grade curriculum, but she must also learn about herself and the true meaning of friendship.

The Paths of Gracie is the quest to live up to the age old statement "be true to yourself." But first one must answer "Who am I?" As Gracie seeks to answer that question, she finds not only her identity but uncovers other insights into relationships with family, friends, and most importantly God.

Tammy Herman
Associate Pastor, Sunrise United Methodist Church

one

GRACE TOOK THE brand new shirt in her hand and hurled it across the room. She smiled with satisfaction as it landed with a thud in a lump on the floor beside her brown wicker chair. She couldn't remember exactly when it had become so important to look good, no, not good, stylish, but it seemed that lately she never looked quite the way she wanted. She wanted desperately to look stylish, especially today, but never felt she actually achieved that look no matter what she did. As she headed back to stare into her closet, she heard her mom.

"Gracie! You need to get down here and eat breakfast before you run out of time!" Bev bit her tongue, almost bringing blood, right after the words were out of her mouth. She knew what was coming next.

Grace breezed into the kitchen, still in the pajamas that had gotten a bit too small over the summer, and snarled at her mom, "I thought I told you not to call me that anymore!"

"I know, and I'm sorry. You're just going to have to give me some time to break my habit, ok?" After a few moments of silence, she repeated, "Ok?"

"Ok! What am I supposed to eat?"

Bev blinked hard, counted to ten a couple of times, and then turned to her daughter, "Cereal always works."

As Grace rummaged through the cabinet, she mumbled under her breath. She could feel her frustration growing and wasn't at all sure if she was going to be able to keep herself from literally blowing up. Today was her first day of eighth grade. It was a very important day, but no one else seemed to care. She was about to finish middle school and then would be in high school. She didn't know what to eat; she didn't know what to wear; and most importantly, she didn't know what the day was going to be like. She was not one to enjoy the unknown. She liked things to be clearly mapped out. Details were important to Grace. Not that she couldn't be spontaneous, she definitely could, just ask her friends, but she didn't like new situations where there were too many unknowns. These induced stress, stress she wasn't quite able to deal with productively this particular morning.

She grabbed a box of cereal, only to discover that Ryan, her brother who was entering third grade, had not closed it. As the cereal flew all around the kitchen, Grace jumped up and down in anger and screamed, "Ryan!! I'm going to kill you!"

Ryan poked his head in from the hallway. His elementary school bus didn't come for hours, and he was raring to go. He looked around at the mess, grinned, and said, "Don't worry. I'll go get Avis."

In a moment, a miniature Beagle came galloping into the room, tail wagging and nose to the floor. With a happy yelp, the tri-colored pooch began to chomp the Cookie Crisp that littered the floor. Grace knew cereal was not healthy for the dog, and she considered making her stop eating, but then she would have to somehow get things cleaned up and still have time to get ready. Making the only logical choice, she let Avis enjoy her snack and turned to grab a bowl. With no bowl or milk mishaps, Grace settled down to eat.

She managed to make it through breakfast, in spite of her mom's constant reminders that she was running late. After placing her bowl in the sink, she charged up to her room, prepared for further battle with her closet. She had been trying for several days to find a special outfit for the first day of school, but she was still undecided. When she ran into her room, Grace was stunned to discover an outfit lying out on her bed. It was perfect! It was dressy enough for this momentous day, but it was also casual enough to look like she wasn't trying too hard. She let out a triumphant howl and hurried to get dressed, for there was more to be done before she could leave the house.

Grace's mom smiled out in the hallway. She knew Gracie, oops, Grace believed, her mom just couldn't understand what she was going through today. The nerves and worries were actually things Grace's mom understood very well, but Grace would never have believed that on this particular morning. This made Bev feel even better about helping her daughter. She had noticed that more and more lately, Grace was shutting her out. Bev remembered when Grace was easy going and easy to get along with, but she knew all things changed. Grace was trying to find her own way. She just hoped that as Grace met the many challenges that lay ahead of her, she would turn to her mom when she needed help. Bev jumped as she heard the sound of a comb bouncing off the bathroom mirror.

It was just as Grace had expected. Her hair was not going to cooperate. The thick light brown mop was just going to look like a mop! She was mortified and frustrated. She could hear her mom shuffling down the hall and quickly picked up the comb that had barely missed flying into the toilet. The lid being open was just one more thing she could add to the list of things she wanted to kill her brother for!

"Do you need help with something Grace?" Her mom's voice was surprisingly calm considering the look on her face.

"Only if you can give me some new hair!" Grace answered in a voice that was a bit too loud.

"You've been to this school before, Grace, and your friends will all be there. Is there any special reason why you're so nervous?"

Grace looked at her mom. How had she known how nervous she was feeling? Why did her mom always seem to know how she was feeling when she was just figuring it out herself? She just hated it when that happened. Surely she should know how she was feeling before everyone else did. She finally said, "I just need ten more minutes, and I'll be ready."

Bev retreated as Grace turned back to study the mirror. She had seen all kinds of emotions running across Grace's face and hadn't known for certain what kind of response she was about to get. She wanted Grace to be independent, but she also wished her daughter would talk to her. Bev would have really liked to know what was going on inside Grace's head.

As Grace had said, ten minutes later she descended from her room, hair under control and backpack in hand. She said good bye to her mom, as if she had not a care in the world, and headed down to the bus stop. She thought that maybe the butterflies in her stomach had morphed into grasshoppers as she fought to keep her demeanor casual. She couldn't quite put her finger on the real reason why she was so nervous today. She had attended Patton Elementary School since she started school and was going to complete Patton Middle School this year, then she'd go to Patton High School. The school wasn't new, the people weren't new, even the teachers weren't all going to be new. She knew she was going to have Mrs. Bowman again this year for Spanish and would have Mr. Michael again for math. She was actually looking forward to English class and couldn't wait for band class to begin again. So, she told herself sternly as she reached the corner, you just need to settle down and go with the flow.

Grace hated riding the bus. Since most of the kids in her neighborhood were younger, there was really no one on it for her to talk to. The Smith twins and Tonya from across the street were entering sixth grade, while Bobby, Julie, and Walter were going into seventh. She smiled at them at the bus stop. She had talked to, and even hung out with, some of them over the summer, but everyone knew she was an eighth grader this year and hanging out with the younger kids just wasn't done. The ride to school seemed unending, but Grace finally stepped off the bus and entered her final year of middle school. She didn't know what a remarkable year it was going to be.

THE HALLS OF PATTON MIDDLE SCHOOL SEEMED MORE crowded than Grace had remembered. She vaguely recalled her dad commenting on how quickly the town was growing, but she never considered how that might affect her. She slowly made her way to locker number 134. She anxiously searched the hallway for a familiar, friendly face as she inched her way through the throng of chatty adolescents. As she arrived at her locker and began to work on the lock, she heard a familiar squeal behind her. Grace turned and met her best friend and locker partner with a squeal of her own and a hug.

"I'm sooo glad to see you, Christina!" Grace told her friend. She and Christina Weiss had known each other since they could remember, and had been best friends since they had Mrs. Lewis together in third grade.

"I've been waiting for you to get here, Gracie! Oops, of course I meant Grace. I'm almost as bad as your mom!" Christina said laughing and then she stepped aside so Grace could see the girl standing behind her. "You know Hope Landers, right?"

It really wasn't a question, as the girls had known each other since Hope had moved to town when the girls were in first grade. What the question was, as far as Grace was concerned, was why Hope Landers was standing with Grace Williams and Christina Weiss at their locker while other people were around. They had never fought or been huge rivals or anything like that, but she and Christina had also never really been friends with Hope. Hope ran in a different crowd. Grace had friends who fell into many groups at school. She had never really paid any attention to what group anyone was in, but she had never really associated with Hope's group. They were known as the popular kids; the ones who were pretty, wore nice clothes, always knew just what to say, and always seemed to get what they wanted. She wasn't sure what was going on, but Grace did eventually manage to say, "Of course I know Hope. Hi."

Hope rolled her big, blue eyes, "I wasn't sure if you remembered how to talk. But since you have, hi to you too. Now let's get moving. There are plenty of boys to see and be seen by in these halls."

With a giggle and a toss of her beautiful, long blond hair, Hope turned to walk down the hall. Grace looked after her thinking she'd like to learn to toss her hair like that. Of course, she'd have to grow out her shoulder length hair and dye it blond to get the right effect. Christina gave Grace a tug and set out after Hope. Grace felt more confused than ever as the grasshoppers in her stomach multiplied. With a shrug and a shove for her backpack, Grace closed her locker and set off after her friend, or was it friends? She still wasn't sure about that one.

The three girls walked the halls greeting some people and ignoring others until their numbers grew to seven, then nine, and then twelve. They were making quite a stir, as they caused even more congestion in the already crowded hallways. By the time the bell rang signaling it was time to get to first hour, you could almost hear an audible sigh of relief from the other students as the girls split up to go to class.

Grace couldn't help but notice they didn't all split up. As it turned out, Christina and Hope had very similar schedules, and they walked to class together. Grace tried not to feel jealous. After all, she had other friends too, good friends she enjoyed spending time with, but none of them were quite like Christina. She could tell her anything–absolutely anything. As she stepped into Algebra, she wondered if that were true any more.

Even as she made her way through her first four classes, Grace couldn't quite shake the feeling that things were not as they should be. She had gotten seat assignments, textbooks, and first day information sheets filled out and now it was lunchtime. She had always loved this break in the day. It was a time to talk with friends, laugh, take a walk outside if the weather was nice, and maybe even eat a little lunch. Today, she felt a bit apprehensive as she walked through the doors into the cafeteria. She looked around for Christina. Grace could not remember the last time that the two of them had not eaten lunch together at school, unless one of them was sick. But she wasn't sure what to expect today. They hadn't set up a meeting place as they had in years past, so it took Grace a few minutes to find the right table. When she finally spotted Christina, she felt surprised, and she also felt that same stab of jealousy she had felt earlier that morning. Christina and another friend of Grace's, Brenda Short, were sitting at the table with Hope and all of her friends. Actually, they were occupying two tables, which was lucky for Grace or she may not have had a place to sit. If things weren't going badly enough, of the two seats that were left, neither was at the table where Christina was sitting. As Grace managed to squeeze into the seat next to Brenda, Christina smiled and waved at her. Grace did manage to wave back, but she was pretty sure her attempt at smiling was a failure.

Somehow Grace survived lunch. No one really paid much attention to her. She made eye contact with whoever was speaking, smiled, laughed when appropriate, and couldn't remember one thing that was said when the bell rang to send them on to fifth hour. She actually felt her lips curve into a smile as she thought of getting out of there and getting to her next class.

Grace practically bounded into the band room. She couldn't wait to get back to learning to play the clarinet. She started playing the woodwind instrument in seventh grade and immediately loved it. She discovered that she loved making music as much as she loved listening to it. She scampered back to get her horn out of the instrument closet and almost ran right into someone she didn't know. The girl smiled at her as Grace gaped in return.

"Hi, I'm Jennifer. My family just moved to Patton this summer, so I'm new," said the girl.

"Oh hi. I'm Grace," Grace said quickly and then she walked away. She was focused on getting her horn and getting ready to play. She didn't have time for chatting with newcomers.

As Grace sat down and began to assemble her clarinet, the band teacher approached her and bent down to say, "Hello Grace, I hope you had a good summer, and that you found at least some time to practice."

"Hello, Mrs. Schwear. I practiced at least three times a week all summer long," Grace responded eagerly.

"Good for you, and for us! I want to introduce you to our newest member of the band." As Mrs. Schwear motioned for her, Jennifer walked over. "This is Jennifer Brown. Jennifer, this is Grace Williams. Jennifer is also a clarinet player. I'm going to have her sit by you for now, until we play for chairs later this month."

"Sure, Mrs. Schwear," said Grace even as she wanted to crawl under her chair and hide in embarrassment.

"I think we met," grinned Jennifer, "back there in the instrument closet."

"Great, now you girls have a few moments to get to know one another while we all get ready for rehearsal," and with that Mrs. Schwear hurried off to remedy a tuba disaster.

Jennifer sat down in the chair next to Grace and began putting her clarinet together. Grace knew she should say something, but at that moment she had no idea what that something might be. So she also busied herself with getting ready to play. What a day she was having! What else was she going to have to face on her first day of school?

At supper that night, Bev could tell something was bothering Grace. She couldn't remember her smiling since she'd walked in the door. Right now she was poking at her chicken and barely responding to anyone. Even Ryan couldn't get a rise out of her, which was really unusual. Bev knew Grace had been very nervous that morning, but she had hoped her first day back to school would turn out to be pleasant. It appeared this had not been the case.

"So, Grace, did anything interesting happen today at

school?" Bev braced for a snarl in return. She was happy she hadn't said Gracie.

Grace didn't feel like answering; she didn't feel like doing anything but maybe crawling into a hole and never coming out. She glanced up for only a moment as she answered quietly, "Nothing worth talking about."

This answer was almost worse than a snarl. Now Bev was really worried. She couldn't imagine what had happened today to make Grace so sad, and she couldn't imagine how she was going to find out what it was. She wasn't sure if there'd be a whole lot she could do to help, but she sure hated not knowing.

Grace knew nothing of her mom's dilemma. All she knew was she had to get away from the table. She couldn't face any more questions. She was thinking of going and calling Christina. Maybe they would talk just like they used to last year if no one else was around. She decided that calling was a great idea. Feeling hopeful, she looked up and sounded a bit better as she said, "I'm not really hungry. I think I'll just go work on some stuff."

"You haven't eaten anything," her mom started, and then, throwing up her hands, thought better of it, "Ok, let me know if I can help with anything."

Grace left the table as quickly as possible and practically ran to the phone. She dialed Christina's number as she had hundreds of times before and waited. All she heard was the repeated signal telling her the line was busy. She couldn't help wondering who was talking on the line. She hung up and went upstairs to practice her clarinet and do the homework that her science teacher had the audacity to assign on the first day of school.

The next morning was nearly a carbon copy of the previous one. What to wear, what to eat, how to make her light brown hair look blonder, and all the while Grace worried about what the day would bring. She had lost count of how many times she had tried to call Christina last night, only to get a busy signal. She couldn't believe she had not talked to her best friend about the first day of school! What was happening between the two of them?

As she neared her locker, Grace spotted Christina. She was alone! Things were looking up. Grace picked up her pace and called out, "Hey, Christina!"

Christina looked up and smiled, "Hi, Grace!" You could just barely hear the -ie she cut off Grace's name.

"I tried to call you last night," Grace decided to dive in and find out as much as she could about what was going on between them.

"Oh, I bet the line was busy. Hope called and then Brenda and then Hope again … I was on the phone almost the whole evening, at least that's what my dad was saying!" Christina said with a laugh.

Grace was hurt but tried to cover it up, "Did something happen?"

"Oh no. We were just talking. I was going to call you, but there just wasn't time. Sorry."

"Oh that's all right," Grace lied as the bell rang. "Maybe we can talk at lunch."

"Sure," Christina called back over her shoulder as she joined Hope and headed to class.

Her morning classes and lunch went pretty much as it had the day before, except Grace remembered the conversation this time. Since it was Thursday, the group spent lunch working on plans for the weekend. They couldn't seem to decide between the park and the mall, so the debate was tabled for phone calls later that night. Grace was excited to escape from all of them and go to band class. She didn't realize how lucky she was to have something to pour her frustrated energies into.

The first person Grace saw as she entered the band room was Jennifer. She hadn't noticed yesterday that Jennifer was fairly small, thin and not too tall. Grace felt tall next to her, as she used to feel all the time, until her classmates had caught up with her growth spurt, many of them surpassing her height. Grace knew she had to talk to Jennifer today. Grimly, she grabbed her horn and headed to her seat. As she sat down, she mustered all of her energy to turn and smile at Jennifer.

"Hi, Jennifer. How was your first day of school in Patton?"

"Well, to be honest, I haven't found too many people to be very friendly," Jennifer replied slowly.

Grace was surprised. She had always thought of Patton as a friendly place. Patton was a small town. Most people knew each other, and many people who lived there had lived there all their lives. There were a few people who moved in and out, and that number was steadily growing, but on the whole it was a town where people came and stayed. As Grace thought about it, she guessed that might make it even harder to be a newcomer. She turned to Jennifer.

"I'm sorry I wasn't friendlier yesterday. The day went a

little differently than I had expected. I shouldn't have let that keep me from making you feel welcome."

Jennifer smiled at Grace, a really big, warm smile Grace noted, "I'm so glad you said that! I just thought you didn't like me. I hope you're having a better day today."

Grace didn't get a chance to respond, as Mrs. Schwear stepped up to the podium and started class, but the girls did manage to whisper a bit later while other instruments practiced their parts. Grace was surprised at how easy it was to talk to Jennifer. She learned that this was Jennifer's third new school in five years. Grace didn't know if she would be able to deal with a life like that. At the end of class, the two girls exchanged phone numbers. Grace flashed her first real smile in two days as the girls parted to go to their next classes.

Grace was still smiling as she reached her locker to get her books for Spanish class. Hope and Christina came around the corner.

"Someone has met a guy, and it's only the second day of school! Look at that smile!" Hope said in only a slightly sarcastic tone.

"What? Oh, no. I j-just had a good time in band," Grace stammered.

"Right … band class. Whatever you say," Hope said.

"No, really. I enjoy music," Grace looked at Christina for help.

"Hey don't look at me, I haven't fallen for any cute guys lately," Christina and Hope nearly fell over each other laughing.

Grace felt like she had been kicked in the stomach, but

she tried to cover it up by laughing and saying, "Right guys, you laugh. I have to get to Spanish class."

Grace turned and walked away. She fought desperately to stay at a normal pace when she really wanted to run at top speed. Her mind was spinning as she slumped into her seat in class. She made it through class on automatic pilot and did the same until she got home. All she could think about as she moved through the afternoon was that Christina had sided with Hope and had left her dangling out on her own. She didn't feel like crying because she really didn't feel anything at all. The shock of being betrayed by her best friend would take a while to wear off.

two

weeks of school had finally passed. Grace didn't understand anything that was happening. She felt like she had entered an alternate dimension, and all she wanted to do was go home. She had managed to come up with excuses for not going anywhere on the weekends with Christina and "the group", as she had come to call the dozen or so girls that seemed to flock around Hope. She couldn't understand why those girls, many of whom were barely paid any attention to, were so happy to flit around the outside of the group. She was sitting with "the group" at lunch and hung out with them before school started in the mornings, but Grace just couldn't get used to the weird feeling that at any time she could be cast out of "the group". Worse, she felt like she had lost her best friend. She and Christina hardly ever spoke to each other and never had any time when it was just the two of them.

Bev had been watching Grace over the past weeks and just couldn't put her finger on exactly what she thought was going on. She had noticed a marked decrease in the time Grace spent on the phone, but she had tried to chalk that up to her studying and practicing. She felt sure she could do something to help, even if it was just listen, if Grace would just let her. She had been reading books to try to get ideas on how to help, but none of them had offered anything of real use.

Grace was sitting beside her mom in Calvary Church that Sunday morning as thoughts of these things were running through both of their heads. They sat as a family, as they did every Sunday, with Grace's brother on the end of the pew bent over his Game Boy. Her father sat beside him looking as if he'd like to be bent over a Game Boy, and her mother sat between her and her father listening, trying desperately to hear something that would help. Grace was trying not to yawn as she glanced around the church. She sucked in a breath of surprise as she spotted Jennifer sitting by her mother near the back by the doors. Grace's heart lightened a little. Jennifer had been the only bright spot in her life since school had started. They had a great time together in band and occasionally called each other in the evenings. At the end of the service, Grace grabbed her mom and dragged her toward the back of the church.

"What are you doing Gracie?!" Bev tried to keep her voice low and a smile plastered on her face as she was being wrenched through the crowd.

"There's someone I want you to meet," Grace replied, purposely ignoring her mom's slip up with her name.

At the sound of excitement in her voice, Bev relaxed a bit and allowed herself to be led a bit more easily. Her curiosity had been piqued. In a moment, they were standing in front of a lovely little girl with long brown hair and a big friendly smile. She was with her equally attractive mother. Bev smiled as Grace introduced them.

"Mom, this is Jennifer. You know, from band class. She's a great clarinet player," as Grace said this, she realized that was actually about all she really knew about Jennifer.

"Hi! It's really Grace that's the great player," Jennifer immediately shook Bev's hand. Bev smiled in return and turned to meet Jennifer's mother.

"Hi, I'm Beverly Williams, but please call me Bev."

The mothers finished introducing themselves to each other as the girls stepped aside and began talking. Bev had only heard Grace mention Jennifer a few times, but she was quite glad to meet her and was impressed with Marie Brown. They talked quite easily mom to mom.

"We've only been attending this church for about a month," remarked Marie Brown, "but I was considering joining the small group for parents that meets on Wednesday evenings. Do you know anything about it?"

Bev was quite embarrassed, "Honestly, I didn't even know there was such a group!"

"Well, would you be interested in getting some information and going together?" Marie asked. "Maybe we could work together to understand teenage thinking."

Bev had been invited to different classes before by well-meaning acquaintances and had always declined. Her usual answer was that her family was just too busy and everyone was doing fine, so she had better not. This time she heard herself saying, "I think that would be a great idea! I could use some help with that."

As if in tandem, the two girls were having a very similar conversation.

"I've never seen you here before. How long have you been coming?" Grace asked.

"Oh, I don't know, maybe a month or so. We almost always sit back here since we don't know anyone," Jennifer replied.

"I've been coming to this church for as long as I can remember," Grace said looking around and noticing all the strangers.

"So how's the youth group?" Jennifer asked.

Grace was quite embarrassed, "Honestly, I didn't even know there was such a group!"

"I was planning to go tonight for the first time. Why don't you come with me?"

Grace was a bit stunned. This seemed like a big step to her. "I'll have to talk to my mom, but I'll try."

"Great!" Jennifer said. Both of their mothers called them at that moment.

As they climbed into the car, Grace and Bev had similar thoughts once again, "What have I done?"

Grace wrestled for a while with whether or not to go to church that night, but in the end she didn't go. She decided there were just too many unknowns, and she wasn't up to jumping off another cliff just then. To be on the safe side, she didn't mention the invitation to her parents. She knew her dad wouldn't have made her go; church was just a habit for him. He went to keep up appearances but was usually glad to escape when the hour was up. Her mom, on the other hand, probably would have felt sorry for Jennifer since she was new in town and would have made her go just to be nice. Grace did hope Jennifer would still talk to her in band the next afternoon. She was just going to have to take the chance.

Instead of going to the youth group meeting, Grace sat in her room on her swivel wicker chair stroking Avis' head and pondering how she could make herself be happy again. This year just wasn't starting off the way she had planned. She was supposed to be having a fantastic final year in middle school, but instead she was miserable. She didn't like that Hope seemed to be Christina's new best friend or that Christina hardly ever called her any more. She didn't like that she felt invisible at lunchtime. She didn't like that frequently no one spoke to her as she walked down the halls. How was she going to fix this?

Grace was a fairly shy person, opening up only as she got to know people, but she knew this situation called for some drastic action. She knew she was on her own to come up with a solution that she could successfully carry out. She gave Avis a push and got up to pace as her mind raced with possibilities. She could begin ignoring Christina and maybe she would snap back to being the girl Grace remembered from years past. She could try to come down with some awful illness, and then Christina would feel sorry for her and beg to spend time with her. She could find herself a cute boy to hang out with and then Christina would think she was the cool one instead of Hope. Then Christina would get back to being her best friend.

She knew none of these solutions were likely to come to pass. She was afraid to ignore Christina and maybe never talk to her again. She felt fine. And there's no way she would ever just walk up to a cute boy and start talking to him, let alone hang out with him. So Grace decided she would just have to come up with something else. She paced for a while letting her mind wander.

She finally decided she would have to do whatever was necessary to fit in with "the group". She nodded her head as she continued to pace. She would laugh when necessary, talk when necessary, and go shopping if she had to so she could wear what was necessary. She felt a little better. At least she had a plan. She would begin implementing that plan the very next morning.

Grace got up thirty minutes earlier than usual the next morning. She decided that if she was going to be able to look right, she would need some extra time for primping. She had gone through her closet the night before looking for the perfect outfit. It seemed to her that nearly all of the girls in "the group" wore bright colors and left their hair down to hang straight. Grace dug out an orange shirt she had never worn and then headed for the bathroom to wet down and blow dry her hair, until it surrendered all of its curl.

Bev said nothing when she saw Grace coming down the stairs. She, of course, noticed the orange shirt that Grace had declared months ago she hated and would never wear. She also noticed the havoc the dryer had wreaked on the body in her hair, but she still managed to say nothing as she sipped her coffee at the table. Grace grabbed the Cookie Crisp, but then had second thoughts and exchanged it for her dad's whole grain cereal. She didn't like the taste of this cereal, but she couldn't afford any extra pounds on her 5'4" frame. Bev was surprised she didn't explode, but she still said nothing. Grace finished getting ready and headed to school full of determination.

At her locker that morning, Grace made a point of saying hi to Hope first and then to Christina. She also laughed at all of Hope's ridiculous jokes and oohed and aahed as Hope pointed out particular "BOIS", boys of interest. Grace felt exhausted, but satisfied, as she headed to her first class.

All morning long, Grace tried to prepare herself for lunch. She darted out of her fourth hour class as fast as she could. She had brought her lunch so she didn't have to stand in line today. She walked as quickly as she dared to the cafeteria and spotted the tables where "the group" was gathering. She bravely walked straight to the main table, Hope's table, and took a seat directly across from Hope. Grace started slowly; she had decided it was best to gradually become more involved in "the group" activities. She laughed at jokes a little louder today, and even chimed in with a few remarks of her own. By the end of lunch her face hurt from smiling, but she was satisfied with her performance. Now she headed to band hoping desperately that Jennifer wouldn't be mad at her for not showing up at the youth group meeting last night.

"Hi Grace!" Jennifer greeted her, "Are you ready to play?"

There was no mention of church, or boys, or what anyone was or wasn't wearing that day. Grace was horribly relieved and enjoyed the class.

GRACE AROSE THE NEXT MORNING WITH THE SAME resolve to fix her friend situation and reclaim her happiness.

She took painstaking care getting ready, ate her healthy cereal, and headed into battle. She didn't really feel any happier, but she was convinced her plan would work if she just tried hard enough. She giggled, she pointed, and she walked the halls with girls she barely knew, and by the end of the week, Grace was exhausted. She had worked and worked to say and do the right things all week, but her work was not finished, for on Wednesday she had come up with a great idea. She'd gone straight to her mom.

"Hey, mom, can I have a few friends over Friday night?" Grace tried to act nonchalant about the whole thing, but she felt like her social life hinged on her mother's answer.

"Sure, Gracie, I mean Grace. What did you have in mind?" Bev was excited that Grace seemed to be feeling so much better. She hoped she hadn't ruined anything with her name slip-up.

"Oh, I just thought a few girls could come over and hang out. Maybe watch a movie or something and have pizza and popcorn."

"That sounds fine," her mom's answer made Grace's heart soar with the possibilities.

Grace had immediately headed to the phone and begun dialing numbers. She started with Hope, as she knew this was the one person who just had to come. It took a bit of talking, but Hope eventually said she would come. After she got a yes from Hope, Grace moved on to Christina, then Brenda, and she even invited a girl she barely knew named Yvette. She believed they all sounded excited to come; Grace was flying high. She had a great day at school on Friday, with the only glitch coming at the end of band class when Jennifer had invited her to the youth group meeting on Sunday evening again. Grace had given her some excuse about being so busy over the weekend that she would have to do all of her homework on Sunday evening. She was not going to be distracted from putting her plan into action.

Friday night finally arrived. Grace was a bundle of nerves. After much thought and staring into her closet, she had opted to just leave on her clothes from school, but she pulled her hair back for a more casual look. She was just plumping the pillows on the couch, something she didn't even know she knew how to do, when the doorbell rang. She jumped about a mile high and then sprinted at top speed for the door, trying to get there before her mom. She slipped in just as her mom was reaching out to turn the knob. The first person to arrive was Brenda, and then Hope and Christina arrived together. Yvette got there just as Grace was about to close the door behind Christina. The evening was underway.

The whole evening was a smashing success in Grace's mind. The girls all enjoyed the movie and the popcorn. After the movie, the girls settled in to eat pizza. Grace had planned on the pizza first, but Hope had decided it would be better to save the pizza for last. She had explained that that way they could eat and talk until their parents arrived to pick them up. Everyone had agreed it was a good idea, so that's what they did.

Bev tried to stay out of the way but still keep tabs on what was happening. She had been quite surprised to see who had arrived on their doorstep. She hadn't asked for a guest list because she thought she knew who would be coming. Boy had she been wrong! She had met Hope Landers before but only for a moment, and Yvette was all new to her. The way Grace had been acting was starting to make a little more sense as Bev watched the girls. She wasn't sure she liked how things were going. There was a lot of laughter, but she felt Grace's was forced. She decided to check on them again and accidentally got an earful as she neared the room.

"Did you see that Rebecca Frankie today?" Hope was saying in a disdainful voice, "She looked so bad it was almost scary."

"I can't imagine coming to school dressed like that and then trying to act like it's normal," Christina added with a laugh.

Bev was mildly surprised to hear the girls talking about Rebecca. From what she knew about Rebecca, she thought she was a really nice girl. Grace and Christina had worked with her on a group project in science just last year. From the laughter she had always heard when they'd gotten together to work, they'd had fun and had gotten an A on the project. She wondered what had happened with her for these girls to ridicule her so mercilessly.

Grace was surprised the girls had targeted Rebecca too. She had always liked Rebecca. She and Christina had hung out with her quite a bit last year, and Grace had a class with her this year. She didn't like the turn this conversation had taken. Still, she heard herself saying, "She was dressed like a garage sale flunky."

This comment brought howls of laughter from the other girls. Grace joined in the laughter, but it seemed like hard work. She knew that Rebecca's family didn't have a lot of money, and Rebecca actually did a lot with what she had.

Grace knew Rebecca had learned to sew so she could fix up some of the clothes she had. She had no idea why she had said that horrible thing about her, but she was pleased with the reaction she received.

Bev stopped short in the hallway. Her head was spinning. She couldn't believe what she had just heard. She knew the voice, but the words were foreign. When and why had her Gracie started talking like that? Bev couldn't imagine what was going through Grace's head. She was determined to talk to Grace when the evening was over. She plastered on a smile and walked on into the kitchen to see if the girls needed anything.

Grace saw her mom coming and hoped she hadn't heard what she had just said. Grace watched her as she offered more drinks to her friends, and her hopes were dashed. Her mom was still being very friendly, but her smile seemed a little less genuine. Grace could tell she wasn't completely happy. Now she dreaded the girls leaving, since she knew her mom would try to talk to her. She hated all the questions. She also knew she wouldn't have any good answers. The reason for not having any good answers was something Grace tried not to think about.

The girls talked and laughed for a while longer, Grace not chiming in as often as she had been. It appeared everyone had a good time, even Yvette. Grace wasn't totally sure if she liked Yvette. She seemed a bit rude and tended to interrupt a lot when others were talking, but she was one of Hope's and now Christina's good friends, so Grace had worked to make sure she had a good time.

Yvette's dad came first, and she was very careful to thank

Grace's mom for having her and then, even as she began to giggle, said good bye to everyone else. Brenda's mom arrived before Grace even closed the door behind Yvette. Next was Hope's mom. She came inside to meet Bev.

Mrs. Landers looked almost exactly like Hope. They both had long blond hair, big blue eyes, tanned skin, and very trendy clothes complete with sequined flip-flops and hot pink toe nail polish. They also laughed alike, and as they said good night there was lots of giggling and gushing. Bev was relieved when they finally left. She felt like the two Landers had drained her of all her energy. She wondered even more why Grace had chosen to invite over these particular girls.

That left Christina. Grace was curious to see how she would act with Hope gone. Maybe the old Christina would make an appearance since it was just the two of them. No such luck. Christina rattled on nervously about nothing important while watching out the window. She barely stopped to take a breath, so Grace hardly got to say a word. When her mom pulled up, Christina seemed relieved and made a run for it, taking only a second to say a quick good bye. Grace could barely cover up her disappointment, but she kept her smile in place, something she was getting very good at, and said good night with a laugh. Grace was relieved to close the door on the evening, until she turned around and saw her mom standing looking at her with her arms crossed. Oh man, here it comes, she thought, while wondering if she could make it to the stairs before the inquisition began. She didn't make it.

"Did you have a good time Grace?" her mom asked as she began to clean up cups and pizza boxes.

The question seemed simple enough, but Grace could not

quite place the tone in her mom's voice. "Yes, it was great," her lack of enthusiasm was apparent even to her.

"I wasn't expecting to see Hope Landers in my living room," Bev watched Grace as she spoke.

There was really no question there, so Grace just waited.

"So, I guess she's one of your good friends?" Bev made the statement into a question.

"Yeah, we just started hanging out when school started," Grace felt like a caged animal, and she kept eyeing the stairs.

"Christina seems to know her well," Bev decided to do a little fact finding while she had Grace on the ropes. "Are they good friends too?"

"Yeah, she's the one who first started hanging out with her," Grace didn't look at her mom.

"I wasn't trying to eaves drop," her mom started, Grace groaned on the inside, "but I couldn't help overhearing parts of your conversation. When did you and Rebecca Frankie have a fight?"

"Oh, we've never had a fight," Grace tried to keep her answers brief so she didn't give too much information or get herself into too much trouble.

"You've never had a fight. Then what happened between the two of you?"

"Oh, nothing has happened," Grace looked at the ground. She had some idea what was coming next.

"If you're still friends with her, then how could you talk about her like that? You sounded so mean earlier. I couldn't believe it was you talking," Bev fought to keep her temper in check. She wanted this conversation to continue.

"I didn't really mean any of that," as Grace said it, she knew it was true.

"Then why would you say it? And why would you join in the laughter aimed at hurting someone else?"

"She wasn't here!" Grace's voice started to rise. "She'll never know I said any of that! How will it hurt her if she doesn't even know about it?"

"Does that make it right? Because she doesn't know, does that make it right?" Bev asked the question quietly. Grace did not respond, so Bev continued, "Would you like those other girls to talk about you like that?"

"Of course not!"

"How do you know they don't talk like that behind your back?"

"Oh, mom! I'm their friend! They wouldn't talk about me behind my back!"

"If they are willing to talk about any and everybody else, what makes you so sure they don't talk about you too?"

Grace had never thought about that and wasn't going to start now. "They don't! I know they don't!"

Bev could tell Grace was on the verge of running out of the room. She wasn't sure what to say. Anything she said now was going to be stubbornly ignored. She only had one idea left.

"I know you're going through a tough time right now Grace. I know I don't know everything that's going on, but I hope you take the time to think things through and eventually make the right choices. If you ever need someone to talk to, I will always be here for you. Even if all you want is someone to listen and say nothing, I will be here for you. I want you to know I'll be praying for you. I'll be praying that God will help you find your way," after saying that, Bev didn't wait for a response. She walked quietly from the room.

"You'll pray for me. *You'll pray for me!*" Grace could only stare after her mom as she left the room. She had no idea what had happened to her mother. Since she had started attending those Wednesday night classes with Jennifer's mom, she had turned into some kind of zealot or something. This wasn't the first thing she had done like this either. They had started having to pray before they could eat supper, and Grace had overheard her mom talking to her dad about the two of them praying together or something like that. Grace grinned despite her frustration as she remembered the way her dad had almost fallen out of his chair laughing. She wished she could respond like that. She just got mad. Maybe her mom was just going through some kind of "God phase". She hoped it wouldn't last too long.

Grace headed up to her room. She paused at the top of the stairs as she watched Ryan, who should have been in bed, running at top speed down the hall. He bounced off one wall and barely made the turn into his room without falling down. Grace sighed, thinking that at least she had her own room. She entered her room, closed the door, and sat down on her bed. She started to wonder if her mom could be right about the girls talking about her, but she cut those thoughts short. The only reason she wasn't happy now was because she just wasn't trying hard enough. She decided she would just have to redouble her efforts at fitting in with "the group". She'd definitely have to talk more at lunch and in the mornings as they wandered the halls before classes started, and she would probably have to spend more time on the phone. That might make getting homework finished more difficult, but she would manage somehow. Maybe she could start working on getting to know Yvette and, oh, that other girl that always sat beside Yvette. She couldn't remember her name, but she was going to be one of her best friends. She might also need to spend some more time with "the group" outside of school. Grace was not going to give up, and she went to bed pleased that she had more ideas ready to put into play on Monday.

At church on Sunday, Grace saw Jennifer again, but this time she kept the encounter to a brief hello. Grace didn't want Jennifer to distract her from her plan with invitations to youth groups and things. She considered not talking to Jennifer at all, but since she was fun to talk with during band class, she decided she didn't want Jennifer to be mad at her. She wasn't sure how "the group" would feel about Jennifer, so she would just have to keep that relationship restricted to the band room.

three

GRACE SPENT THE next few weeks doing exactly what she thought would endear her to "the group". She spent so much time remembering to smile, to laugh, to say the right thing at the right time and in the right way that she found herself exhausted every night. Most evenings she barely got her homework finished, sometimes finishing on the bus in the mornings, and she avoided her family.

Bev watched as Grace spent more and more time being someone that none of them knew, or even liked. She had heard Grace on the phone a number of times talking about people and laughing about things that were mean but not funny. She had watched Grace go through her closet and reject all of the clothes she used to love. She had watched Grace be even meaner than usual to her little brother and completely ignore her parents. She had also watched Grace be almost rude to Marie's daughter, Jennifer, whenever they ran into her. Grace seemed to be working to keep Jennifer at arm's length for some reason. Bev knew Jennifer had been inviting Grace to the youth group meeting at church on Sunday evenings. She thought that could be the answer she had been praying for every day. She just didn't know if Grace would ever cooperate. She also didn't know how to respond to Grace's latest request.

"Oh, come on Mom. It's the mall. You've let me go there with friends hundreds of times," Grace didn't like the whiny sound of her own voice, but she felt it was time for her to start spending some weekend time with "the group", and she didn't want her mom to mess things up.

Bev looked at Grace. She thought the "hundreds" of times was a stretch, but she had allowed her to go to the mall by herself with friends in the past. She wasn't sure she could come up with a really good excuse for not letting her go. She didn't think Grace was going to accept that she simply didn't want her to go there with Hope.

"I'll have to talk to your father, and we'll see," was the best she could do for the moment.

"I need to know by tomorrow! I have to tell them tomorrow!" Grace ran up the stairs on the verge of frustrated tears.

Bev took a moment to calm down and then went to find her husband. Charles was in the basement watching television. Bev wasn't sure what he would say, but she had to talk to him since she had said she would.

"Charles, I need to talk to you a minute."

Grace's dad laid down the remote, though he left the TV on, and looked at Bev, "What's up?"

"Grace wants to go to the mall on Friday night …"

"Well, that's no problem. I'll be home late from work, but I could pick her up," he turned back to the TV and began flipping channels again.

"She wants to go with Hope Landers and these other new friends she's been hanging out with at school. I'm just not sure it's a good idea," Bev was feeling frustrated.

"Well, she has to have a chance to make her own mistakes."

Bev wanted to scream. She knew that, but she didn't think setting her up was the way to go either and that's what she felt like she was doing, "I'm afraid these girls could get her into real trouble."

Charles looked up at Bev and said calmly, "We have to trust her."

Well, that was that. Bev knew she had lost, just as she had expected she would. She hoped Gracie would use her common sense and stay out of trouble. She went to deliver the news.

Grace couldn't believe her parents had said yes! She couldn't wait to tell Hope, Christina, and "the group" that she would be going with them on Friday night. She wasn't totally sure what they would be doing, but it was enough for her just to know she would be with them. She felt this was a huge step in solving all her problems.

Wardrobe was a huge problem when Friday night finally arrived. Grace knew she had to change from her school clothes. It was what to change into that was the problem. She finally went with basic jeans and a nice shirt with her hair down and as straight as she could get it. She was so nervous that the car ride to the mall almost made her sick.

"Now, your father will pick you up right by the doors at the main entrance. Do you have your watch?" Grace stuck her arm up so Bev could see. "Good. Don't be late. Have a good time, and use your head."

"Sure, Mom. See ya later," Grace climbed out of the car and into her first night out with "the group".

They all met by the fountain in the center of the mall. Grace was relieved to see she was not the first one there. She didn't want to appear to be too eager. She walked up to the girls already gathered and waited with them for the others to arrive. She didn't really know the girls too well, but she was excited to start the evening.

After Hope arrived, the group of about twelve girls began to walk around. They were quite loud, and they got lots of looks from others, some smiles and some smirks. Grace was having a pretty good time just walking and looking at things. This went on for quite some time, until Hope announced she was bored.

This announcement brought on lots of chattering, and "the group" just stopped where they were, in the middle of the walkway, to discuss other possible activities. Grace stood uncomfortably and listened. She was afraid to offer any suggestions. She just didn't know what these girls usually did when they were out.

Finally, it was Hope herself who came up with the winning idea. They all decided they would play a daring game. Someone would start by daring someone else to do something, and then if the person completed the dare, they could choose who had to go next. Everyone was very excited. Hope, of course, would hand out the first dare.

Grace could barely breathe as she tried to stand where Hope couldn't see her. She hoped no one would notice her trying to hide. Once again, her thoughts were about what she had gotten herself into.

Hope looked around the group. She seemed to be enjoying the drama of taking a long time to choose who would go first. She looked from one person to another and finally spoke.

"Alright, I think Yvette will get to go first!"

There were groans and screams. Yvette didn't seem nervous at all as she walked up to stand by Hope. She smiled as she turned to hear her dare.

"Ok, Yvette, you are going to get a fun one!" Hope started, "I dare you to walk over to that group of high school boys and introduce yourself and shake their hands."

Everyone cheered. Grace couldn't imagine having to walk up to a group of guys, especially high school guys, and talking to them like it was no big deal. She was intensely relieved Hope had not singled her out for the dare.

Yvette made a few remarks about how easy this dare was and then she headed over to meet the guys. Grace watched as the guys turned to look at Yvette when she walked up and then each one shook her hand. Yvette walked back over with a smile on her face. "The group" cheered loudly. Grace wanted to disappear.

Yvette made someone walk up to a security guard and try to get him to help her look for her lost lunch box. Grace kind of felt sorry for the guy because he did try to be nice and offered to find her someone who could help her. The next girl had to stand by the fountain and sing a song. She got lots of applause and laughter. Then the dares started to get even more questionable.

The next girl had to take off her shoes and socks and stand in the fountain for fifteen seconds. She barely got out before a security guard turned the corner. Then she made someone stand outside the toy store and cry for her dolly.

Grace was wishing the floor would swallow her up. Everyone else seemed to be having a good time. Why couldn't she? She actually knew the answer to that question. She didn't want to get in trouble. She didn't want to scare the kids in the toy store. She didn't want to play this game anymore. She was relieved when they finally headed to the food court for a snack. Her relief was short-lived.

A girl named Robin had been the one who had cried in front of the toy store. As they reached the food court, she stopped the group.

"It's my turn to hand out a dare," she seemed to study "the group" for the perfect victim. "Grace, I think I'll dare you."

Everyone cheered as Grace stood rooted to her spot. She could barely breathe. What was she going to do? Someone finally gave her a shove, and she was propelled to the front of the group. She clasped her hands together so the others wouldn't see them shaking.

"Grace," Robin continued, "I've got a great dare for you. I dare you to go stand by the McDonald's counter. You have to stand there and take someone's fries off their tray. You can't come back without fries."

Grace couldn't swallow and her vision was a little blurry. As the others laughed and cheered, she tried to get her brain to start working on her newest problem. She slowly inched her way over to the counter. She stood there wondering how she was going to get out of this without becoming a thief.

Grace knew everyone was watching her. She could feel their eyes on her. She knew this was some kind of test. If she went back empty-handed, they would all laugh at her, and she was sure to lose her lunch seat. She was determined not to steal, so she decided to follow her mom's advice and use her head. It took her several minutes of standing there to finally come up with a solution. When it came to her, she smiled and felt her vision clear a little.

She waited until there was no line, and then Grace ordered some fries, which she asked them to put on a tray. She picked them up off the tray and walked back over to "the group" with a smile still on her face.

"You can't come back. You haven't completed your dare! Or are you too afraid?" Robin tried to sound like she was talking to a baby.

"I completed the dare," Grace said simply as she nibbled a fry.

"How do you figure that?" Robin asked.

"You said to take fries off someone's tray and bring them back here. I did. Here are the fries," Grace held them out for everyone to see.

"You didn't take them off someone's tray, so they don't count," sneered Robin.

"You said to take them off someone's tray. You didn't say whose. It just worked out that the "someone's" tray was my tray," Grace hoped with all her might that her ploy was going to work.

Someone started to laugh, Grace thought it might have been Christina but she wasn't sure, and soon everyone agreed that Grace had completed her dare. They swooped into the food court. Grace was relieved and happy with how things had worked out. She took her fries and sat down with the rest of "the group". They snacked and talked until it was time for their parents to pick them up.

Bev got very vague, one-word answers to her questions when Grace got home that evening. She decided she would probably never know what had happened at the mall that night. She was just relieved things appeared to have worked out.

Grace was hopeful that her Friday night success might make things better at school on Monday. She was disappointed to discover things were exactly the way they had been the week before, and the week before that, and the week before that. She put on her smile and got down to work.

On the following Thursday evening, Grace sat in her room staring out the window and wondering about things. She was starting to feel drained. How long could she keep up this laughing, gossiping, and ignoring everything and everyone else? She was having trouble always remembering who she should or shouldn't talk to, and she couldn't get what had happened today out of her mind.

Hope and Christina had turned the corner in the hallway after second hour and had seen her talking and laughing with

Rebecca Frankie. The two girls had given her a cold stare and walked by without saying a word. Grace had tried to explain at lunch that she was just being nice. She had then proceeded to start making fun of Rebecca in every way imaginable. She couldn't remember everything she had said, thank goodness, but she knew she had mentioned Rebecca's clothes, hair, laugh, and she thought that maybe she had even said something about her teeth. The girls at the table were practically rolling and crying with laughter, and Hope was giving her an approving look. Grace was about to say something else when she noticed someone standing behind the table staring at her. At first she didn't give it much thought and kept on talking, but then she looked up again. She felt like someone had knocked the wind out of her when she realized it was Rebecca who was standing there, staring at her, and listening.

The rest of lunch had been a blur as Grace had fought off a feeling of nausea. She was mortified. No one else at the table seemed to notice, or at least to care about, what had happened. She ran into the band room when the bell rang as if it were a haven. She was happy to see Jennifer and gave her a big smile as she slumped into her chair. This was the first time Grace could remember her not smiling back. She thought Jennifer actually looked distressed.

"Grace, I like you. I believe you are a very nice person, but I also believe you need to do some thinking about what you're doing," Jennifer was not one to beat around the bush. "You really hurt Rebecca's feelings today. I don't know everything you said, and I don't have any idea why you said them. Why would you do that? Do you even know why you said what you did?"

Grace could not come up with a real answer, "I can't believe she heard me. I would never have said any of that if I had known she was standing back there."

"But you would have said it otherwise? That is just as bad. What did Rebecca do to deserve you talking like that about her, whether she hears you or not?" Jennifer was speaking softly and sincerely.

"Well, nothing of course," Grace began, but then she didn't know what else to say that would make any sense.

"Right," said Jennifer, "I want you to know you are still invited to the youth group meeting on Sunday. I really hope you'll come. I think you'd really like it," Jennifer saw Grace about to answer and knew it would be another excuse not to come, so she quickly added, "You can wait and let me know tomorrow or even Sunday morning at church."

Grace said nothing as Mrs. Schwear started rehearsal. She couldn't quite figure out what had happened here with Jennifer. It was obvious Jennifer did not like the way she had talked about Rebecca, but instead of yelling or screaming or anything, she just invited her to a youth group meeting just like every other week. She wasn't so sure she would have been as nice. She also wasn't sure what excuse she would give tomorrow to not go to the meeting this time. Since Jennifer invited her every single week, she was running short on excuses. She hadn't told her she had to stay home and wash her hair yet, but it might be all she could come up with by tomorrow afternoon.

Somehow Grace had survived the rest of the day, and now here she sat, staring out the window. She knew she should be thinking about how Rebecca was feeling. She should be worried about how upset Rebecca was and how mean she had been. She should be worried about how she was going to apologize, but all she could do was think about how badly she herself was feeling. She didn't really understand the rules with her friends any more. She wasn't feeling any happier than she had been when she first began implementing her plan to fit in. Why weren't things getting better? If today was any indication, things were actually getting worse.

THE NEXT DAY AT SCHOOL, GRACE HAD HER EXCUSE ready for Jennifer in band, walking the dog was important and she should take her turn, and she had her smile plastered on for the benefit of everyone else. She still wasn't sure what would happen when she saw Rebecca in English class, but she was planning to just avoid her for a while.

Her classes seemed to be harder lately. Grace had always gotten good grades, and she was still doing well, but she just couldn't seem to focus. Pop quizzes were throwing her into panics and tests always seemed a little more difficult than expected. She just didn't seem to have the time or the energy to study much these days. School had turned into a place to work on fitting in with others, instead of a place to learn things necessary for her future.

The morning passed quickly, and Grace didn't have to worry about avoiding Rebecca because Rebecca wouldn't even look at her. Grace was relieved to be out of English, but now she had to prepare herself for lunch. She had a little more time than usual today since she had to stand in line. She had left her lunch on the counter at home and her mom had refused to bring it, so today she was buying. When she finally got her tray and headed to the table, she just caught the end of a conversation at another table she was passing.

"Yeah, there goes Grace. She used to be so nice. We even talked now and then in class. This year, no one else exists but Hope Landers."

"We used to hang out some, and I always hoped to get to work on a project with her. I don't think I'd want to do that anymore. She's different this year," said someone else who sounded familiar.

Then another voice, "I know. I don't know what happened to her, but I hope she's happy where she is 'cause I don't want her coming over here!"

Grace couldn't quite place the voices, and she didn't dare turn around and look as she heard everyone at the table break into laughter. She sat down in her now usual spot across from Hope. She looked at her food, but all she could think about was what she had heard. She couldn't imagine why anyone would talk about her like that. She was still nice. She still liked to talk to people. She just didn't have time to talk to that many other people anymore. It took all of her energies and time to come up with things to say to "the group". How thin did people think she could stretch herself? She couldn't be all things to all people, could she? With the reassuring thought that she was really doing the best she could, Grace began to eat her lunch. As she talked, she kept a sharp eye on who was around.

Finally band class! It was getting to be the only class Grace looked forward to anymore. She looked for Jennifer. When she didn't see her, she was surprised at how disappointed she felt. That feeling passed quickly, as Jennifer came rushing in just before the bell rang.

"Long line in the bathroom," she whispered with a smile as she sat down and readied to play.

Grace was ready with her excuse for not going to the youth group meeting, but, at the last minute, she decided to wait and tell Jennifer Sunday morning at church. She wanted to just relax and have fun right now. She didn't want any conflict to interrupt the music today.

Grace was thankful for the weekend. She needed a break. All she wanted to do was lie around and watch TV. Unfortunately, Ryan had gotten to the TV in the family room before she did. Since Grace wasn't in the mood for power rangers, she headed downstairs where her parents usually watched TV. Grace stopped short at the bottom of the stairs. There sat her mom, curled up on the couch reading the Bible! Grace tried to quietly turn and sneak back up the stairs, but it was too late.

"Grace, come on down," her mom said.

"Oh, I don't want to bother you," she tried for the stairs again.

"You aren't bothering me. Come on down."

She was caught. She could leave, but then her mom might make her come back or she might follow her. All Grace could do to avoid trouble was walk slowly over to a chair and sit down. She made a quick grab for the remote, but she wasn't quick enough.

"I was just reading, Grace. Did you know there's a proverb that says parents shouldn't frustrate their children?" seeing Grace perk up, Bev quickly added, "Of course, it says that right after it says children should obey their parents."

"Of course," said Grace, once again trying to just turn to the TV for escape.

Bev was determined, "Would you like to look at it with me? I'd love to hear your thoughts on some of these."

Grace didn't want to so badly she could almost taste it. "Sorry mom, I think I'd better get back upstairs and do some homework. I'll leave you to your proverbs."

Bev watched Grace race up the stairs, almost falling in her haste. She was at a complete loss on how to get through to her. She worried about her constantly, even though she knew it was a waste of time and energy. She had learned that God would answer her prayers, one way or the other, in His own time. She just didn't know what to do in the meantime.

Bev reached over and picked up the phone. She dialed Marie Brown's number. She could only hope her new friend might have some ideas. As it turned out, Marie did have an idea. It was an idea Bev had been considering for a while now. She suggested that Bev make Grace go to the youth group meeting on Sunday evening and maybe even have her attend Sunday school before church. They agreed that Grace could really use some sort of positive influence. Marie also reminded Bev that Jennifer had been inviting Grace to go with her to the youth group every week, so there would be someone there she knew. Bev was excited to have some sort of action to take, but she wasn't sure how Grace was going to like it.

It turned out that Grace didn't take Bev's announcement quite as badly as Bev had expected. Grace did put up a fight, at first. She yelled a bit, ran to her room, slammed a door, but then said she would go. It seemed to Bev that Grace just went through the motions of protesting. Bev felt hopeful that she would actually like the group and would learn things that would help her.

Grace sat in her room, once again staring out the window and wondering. She couldn't believe her mom was going to "make" her go to the youth group meeting. What did her mom even know about the group? How did she know they weren't going to try to brain wash her or something? She sighed. At least there was a bright spot, Jennifer would be there. Grace enjoyed their talks in band more than she would admit to herself, so she looked forward to seeing Jennifer in another setting. The weekend was not going as she had planned, but she had to admit that this new twist had its possibilities.

Saturday flew by, and suddenly Bev found herself sitting in church with her family. They had only come to church, Bev had decided not to push her luck by trying Sunday school in the same week she was mandating youth group. She had started doing various small volunteer jobs around the church, so when the service ended she had several people come up to talk with her. She couldn't believe how much more a part of things she felt and how much happier helping out made her. She prayed for the same feelings for Grace.

Grace did notice that more people were talking to her mom after church these days. She found it intriguing but also annoying. She could tell her dad felt the same way as he just got up and headed out the door to wait for them in the car. Grace wanted to get home too. She felt she needed some time to get herself mentally prepared for the meeting that night. She had no idea what to expect, and she didn't want the unknowns to cause her to make a fool of herself.

Grace spent the afternoon pacing her room and staring out the window. She could admit that she was a little excited to see what would happen at the meeting that night, but, more than excited, she was nervous. It was hard to accept that she had no choice about whether or not to go, but she did look forward to seeing Jennifer. She finally lay down on her bed trying to rest, as she watched the clock tick off the minutes until time to go.

Grace entered the church that evening feeling nervous and wary. She still couldn't believe she was here. She fought a feeling of panic as her mind whirled through a list of unknowns: where should she go, who would be there, what would they make her do? She was relieved to see Jennifer when she finally found the right room, but she couldn't figure out why she would sit so close to the front. Grace never went straight for a seat where someone might really notice her, or worse yet, ask her to say something. None the less, Jennifer was the only person Grace really wanted to sit with, so she walked up and joined her.

The evening was surprisingly pain free. Grace did have to introduce herself, but so did everyone else. They read and discussed a story from the Bible. It happened to be a story she was familiar with about a man who got beat up on his way somewhere, and no one would help him but this Samaritan. The Samaritan was a man who usually would have tried to avoid the man who was hurt, but he could not just walk by someone who needed help, even though others did. As they discussed the story, no one ever called on anyone. It was strictly volunteers who did the talking. Nearly everyone participated, including Jennifer. Grace was surprised. She had class with some of these people, and they never spoke. She was also surprised at how much she enjoyed listening to everyone talk about a story she had heard a thousand times and make it seem to have meaning to her life. She went home feeling better than she had in weeks. If only the feeling could have lasted.

four

GRACE REACHED over and hit the snooze button for a second time. She just couldn't seem to find the energy to force herself out of bed. It was comfortable and safe there under the covers. She didn't have to smile if she didn't feel like it, and she didn't have to say anything mean to or about anyone. Grace wanted to hold on to the warm feeling she left church with last night. She pulled the covers up over her head as the alarm sounded again. She was about to hit the snooze for a third time when she heard Ryan bound noisily down the hallway.

She knew if Ryan was up, the rest of the household would be up soon, whether they wanted to be or not. As if on cue, Avis started barking. Grace got up to face the day.

Grace was having trouble getting ready. This really wasn't out of the ordinary, but it seemed worse today. What to wear was an endless problem, but today she also couldn't get the toothpaste out of the tube or find her shoes. She hadn't put her homework into her backpack, so she had to track that down too. As it ended up, Grace missed the bus. Her mom made no secret about how she felt about this.

"Monday mornings are hard enough, Grace. You need to be more organized so this doesn't happen," Bev pulled the car into the drop-off line in front of the school.

Grace decided it was best to say nothing. Deep down, she knew she had no good reason for being late. She just didn't feel like going to school today. She looked glumly out the window thinking it was too bad that feeling didn't come with a fever.

As she slammed the door on her mom's six-year-old car, Grace glanced up just in time to see Hope and Christina try to stop laughing. She looked around a bit trying to find what they were laughing at but didn't see it. She waved to them, hoisted up her backpack, and headed for her locker. She still wouldn't say she felt chipper, but she thought she'd make it through the day.

Even as she walked down the hall, Grace couldn't stop thinking about the story they had discussed last night at the youth group meeting. Just as they were wrapping up, the adult group leader, Mr. Fuller, gave them a challenge for the week ahead. They were challenged to be a good Samaritan to some-one, at least once this week. They were supposed to try to help someone they usually would have tried to avoid. Grace didn't know why she kept thinking about it. She wasn't even sure she would be going back to the group next week, but she just kept thinking it would be fun to help someone like that. She tried to discreetly keep an eye out for anyone needing help as she made her way through the hallways.

Grace was rewarded for her vigilance just after second hour. As she was leaving history class, she spotted a younger student just outside the room surrounded by papers. Grace took a deep breath and walked up to the boy.

"Could I help you with some of this?" Grace reminded herself to smile, but she already was.

"Why would you want to help me?" the boy asked warily.

"Well ..." Grace tried to think fast, "it looks like you've got yourself a big mess here, and if we don't get it picked up soon it's going to start walking away," she pointed to a paper that was stuck to another student's shoe.

"Oh, thanks," said the boy, "sorry I sounded so suspicious. I thought you might be teasing me because everyone else just passed right on by."

His words hit Grace right in the heart. They were almost exactly like the words in the Bible story they read last night. All of those people had passed by that guy on the other side of the road. She felt great! She was being the Samaritan. Grace couldn't remember the last time she had felt so light and happy. She talked with the boy as she helped him pick up the papers. She found out he was in seventh grade and his name was Michael Leest. They had quite a little conversation as they each made a pile of papers in front of them. It turned out Michael had the same teacher for science this year that

Grace had last year. It appeared Mr. Gardener was still using the same jokes this year, as Grace could give the punch line for every joke Michael started. When they finally finished picking up all the papers Grace turned to go.

"Grace, thanks a lot. Not everyone would stop and take the time to help someone out, especially someone they didn't know," Michael smiled at her as he brushed back his too-long bangs and pushed up his glasses.

"I'm really glad I could help you out, Michael. I'll see you around," and with that, Grace hurried off to third hour. She was going to have to move it, or she was going to be late.

Grace was in a great mood the rest of the morning. She couldn't stop smiling, but her face didn't hurt! There was a pop quiz in third hour that brought her down just a bit, but she was still enjoying the feeling she had gotten from simply helping someone. She was in such a good mood she almost forgot to avoid Rebecca in English class. As she headed for lunch, for just a split second, Grace thought it would be fun to sit somewhere else, but she shook off that thought and headed for her spot across from Hope. Within moments, her face started to hurt.

Through most of lunch, Grace just let her mind wander. She had learned if she just smiled and laughed when everyone else did, she didn't really have to pay too much attention to what was actually being said. As she smiled, Grace went back over her morning. As she thought about her adventure at being a good Samaritan, Grace's forced smile instantly became genuine. She wondered if the guy in the story had felt as good as she did, but then she remembered the youth group leader saying it was a story Jesus had told to make a point about how we should help others, even those we don't really like. She had to hand it to Jesus! Helping others was the way to go.

"Now what could our Grace be thinking about?" Christina drawled, "Maybe she's thinking about little Michael Leest after spending that quality time with him this morning."

Grace hadn't realized everyone had gotten quiet and was looking at her. She found she wasn't surprised anymore that it was Christina who was talking about her in that teasing tone of voice. She could feel her cheeks getting red, "I'm sorry. I'm tired. Did I miss something?"

"Why don't you tell us about your new man, Grace?" This time it was Hope talking.

"Are you talking about Michael? I was just trying to help someone," Grace tried not to sound nervous.

"It looked like you were having quite a time 'helping' someone," everyone started laughing at Hope's comment.

"We just t-talked as we picked up his stuff," Grace was mortified that she was starting to stammer. She was confused on how helping someone could cause her to be teased like this.

Grace was so relieved when the bell rang she could have broken into song. She hopped up from the table and raced to band class. She was looking forward to seeing Jennifer and telling her about her Samaritan adventure. She hoped telling Jennifer would turn it back into something good. Something she felt like "the group" was trying to take away from her.

Jennifer had a huge smile on her face as she sat down next to Grace. The girls had been relieved they were still sitting next to each other, even after Mrs. Schwear had seated them in order of ability. Grace was seated first, and Jennifer was right after her. Grace looked up at Jennifer with a grin on her face.

"I saw you this morning," Jennifer said.

Grace's smile disappeared. Was Jennifer going to make fun of her too? She hadn't realized how much she had been counting on Jennifer to understand and even to be happy for her. How could she have been so wrong? Why had she stopped to help Michael? She couldn't believe this was happening.

As Grace's imagination ran away with itself, Jennifer looked up and saw her face, "I didn't mean anything bad," she said quickly, "I thought you might be excited about what happened. Weren't you doing your good Samaritan challenge?"

"Yes!" Grace let out a whoosh of air in relief, "It was great! Did you see it? There were papers everywhere! I barely made it to third hour on time."

"I'm so happy for you! I hope I get my chance sometime this week."

"Oh, I have no doubt," Grace had a great hour.

Grace sort of avoided Hope and Christina for the rest of the day. She didn't really spend a lot of time with them after lunch anyway since their schedules were so different, but today she just sort of made sure she didn't run into them at her locker either. If she had been honest with herself, she would have said it was because she didn't want to ruin her good mood, but she convinced herself it was just to avoid any more teasing.

Bev couldn't help but notice Grace was humming when she came through the door! She couldn't believe it! She wondered what had happened at school. She greeted Grace as she came in, and Grace actually answered her with enthusiasm in her voice. Oh, how Bev prayed things were turning around for Grace.

Grace hung on to the good feeling she'd discovered that morning for as long as she could. She thought that maybe she had finally found a way to make herself happy. All she had to do was keep doing what she was doing and be nice to someone when they needed help. That was easy! Grace kept her smile through supper and even into the next morning, but it became harder to hold onto as she reached her locker and began her Tuesday performance.

Grace's confusion increased with each passing day. She thought she had finally discovered the secret to her happiness, but it seemed to have slipped right through her fingers. She knew she had been happy when she had helped Michael in the hallway with his papers. She also knew if she could just manage to be what her friends wanted her to be that she could be happy with them too. She just wished she could get everything happening at the same time, so her happiness would last. Maybe she would talk to Jennifer about it.

It surprised Grace that she was considering talking to Jennifer about her unhappiness. The only person she had ever shared those kinds of things with was Christina. Last year the two of them would have already spent great amounts of time discussing and analyzing why Grace wasn't happy. This Grace, the unhappy one, had talked to no one about her feelings. Grace was still trying to hang on to her friendship with Christina, while keeping her friendship with Jennifer restricted to the band room. She decided, however, to make an allowance for Sunday evening youth group meetings. She had such a good time at the last meeting, she was actually looking forward to the one this week. Maybe they could give her an idea on how to hang on to the happy feeling she had experienced Monday morning.

Just like every other week, on Friday Jennifer invited Grace to the youth group meeting that weekend. Grace gave her a smile. "You don't have to keep inviting me. I'm actually looking forward to it this week."

Jennifer's smile was huge. "I'm so glad to hear that! I really look forward to the meetings each week, too. I learn so much about myself and about God."

Grace glanced around to see if anyone was listening to them. She wasn't used to talking about God in front of everyone. Of course, she wasn't used to talking about God anywhere else either. Her mom had started trying to talk about God around the house some. Grace thought she was going a little overboard, and she thought Jennifer sounded a little like her mom. She smiled a bit uncomfortably as class ended, and she told Jennifer she would see her on Sunday. What had she gotten herself into? Was she going to start sounding like some kind of Bible thumping crazy?

Grace forgot her worries as she sat next to Jennifer on Sunday evening. This discussion was almost better than last week's. The story they were talking about this week was another one Grace had heard many times in Sunday school when she was little. It was the parable of the prodigal son. She wasn't entirely sure what "prodigal" meant, but the story was about a son who had demanded his inheritance from his father, and then had taken that inheritance and spent it like a crazy man. Grace couldn't quite understand why the father gave the son his money, or why the son spent it on things Grace couldn't even think about. She'd always wondered about that, but she wouldn't have to wonder any longer. She was actually beginning to understand the story.

Mr. Fuller was filling in the gaps as the group discussed and debated. He said that we could think of the father as being God and the son as being each one of us. He said people tend to go out into the world God has given us and do lots of dumb stuff, sort of like the son took the money and squandered it. We all hurt other people and we all hurt ourselves, but he said we can always come back to God, sort of like the son came back to his father. He will always forgive us when we ask, if we are truly sorry, as the father forgave his son in the story.

Grace thought about the son in the story. After he had squandered away everything his father had given to him, he worked feeding pigs for someone. She thought that sounded gross and was glad when the son finally decided going home and being his father's servant would be better than staying where he was. When the son returned home, the father was overjoyed to see him and took him back as his son, not as his servant. The father simply forgave the son and rejoiced that he was home. It all sounded a little too easy to Grace.

To Grace's own surprise, she raised her hand and said just that. Mr. Fuller smiled and said it did sound easy because it is just that easy. God will forgive us if we are sorry and if we ask Him for forgiveness. He didn't try to make things difficult. God wants to forgive us. Then Mr. Fuller gave them their challenge for the week.

"I would like for all of you to go home and think. Think if there is anything weighing on your hearts you need to ask God to forgive you for. You may find you need to go and apologize to someone. You may need to ask a friend, a family member, or even a stranger to forgive you for something that you've done, either intentionally or unintentionally. Then, once you've cleared the decks, so to speak, go to the Lord in prayer. Your challenge for this week is to offer your sins up to the Lord. Ask Him for forgiveness. Hand him your baggage, and He will run out to meet you and take you into His arms of mercy, just like the father in the story."

Grace wasn't so sure about this challenge. The last one had been so easy. Go help someone else you wouldn't normally help. It had been a great experience, but it had been easy. This time, she was supposed to do something for herself. If she thought about it too much, she might even have to talk to other people about mistakes she had made. No, she wasn't excited about this one.

All the way home from the meeting Grace was quiet. Bev wanted to ask her a million questions, but she felt it would be better to leave Grace alone with her thoughts. Instead, Bev said a silent prayer that whatever Grace was thinking about would take her another step toward being truly happy.

Grace wasn't enjoying her thoughts. She couldn't understand why her mom wasn't asking the customary questions. She always wanted to know what they had talked about, who was there, had she learned anything, etc. She would have actually welcomed the interruption from her thoughts, even though she didn't want to answer the questions. Grace already had a few ideas on what she was going to have to do to meet this week's challenge. She hoped she could do the right thing.

five

GRACE MET MONday morning with a yawn. She sat up and stretched and tried not to think too much about the challenge she was facing this week. Maybe she wouldn't have to take part in this challenge. Grace had noticed when they discussed last week's challenge at the youth group meeting that not everyone seemed to have participated, or at least not everyone volunteered information about whom they helped. She looked at her reflection in the mirror and made a face at herself. She had been one of those people. She had loved meeting last week's challenge, but she still hadn't been ready to discuss it with everyone at the meeting.

"Well, there goes that idea," Grace muttered to herself as she faced her closet. Grace knew her conscience wouldn't let her off the hook anyway. For some reason, she really enjoyed these challenges and how they made her feel inside. Somehow, she'd have to figure out what she had to do.

The discussion last night had questions bubbling up in Grace's head. She wasn't sure where she should go to find the answers to these questions. She couldn't really even put her questions into words yet. She could ask her mom. She knew her mom would be very excited to help her with her questions, but she might be too excited. Grace wasn't sure she was ready for just how happy her mom would be to help her.

Another option was asking Jennifer. Grace wasn't positive Jennifer would have any more answers than she had, but she did feel Jennifer was a little ahead of her in understanding God and Jesus and all that Bible stuff. She was already having problems keeping her friendship with Jennifer from extending beyond band class and youth group, so Grace wasn't sure she wanted to ask her either. How could she keep the kind of friendship with Jennifer she wanted if she asked her all kinds of personal questions?

It seemed to Grace that she only really had one option. She was a bit scared, but she thought when she got home from school she might just have to try it. She knew she had a Bible somewhere in her room. She was pretty sure it was in the storage bench at the foot of her bed. When she got home that afternoon, she'd just have to dig it out and see if she couldn't find some answers on her own. Grace was satisfied with her decision, so she finished getting ready and headed to school.

Grace felt like the day was a fairly typical Monday. The bus was late dropping her off at school, so she had to run to first hour. Then at lunch, not one, but two people dropped their trays in the middle of the cafeteria floor. Since it was spaghetti Monday, it wasn't a pretty mess. Grace tried not to laugh at the poor students who did the dropping, but she couldn't keep the smile off her face. She walked over and sat down. Hope, Christina, and "the group" were laughing and calling out things to the embarrassed boys who were trying to clean up their messes. Grace wanted to tell them to be quiet, but, instead, she just sat quietly and ate her lunch.

When Grace got home that afternoon, she ran straight to her room and tore into her storage bench. It didn't take her long to find the Bible the church presented to second graders each year. She had never really looked at it, so the first thing Grace had to do was look it over and figure out how to find what she was after. She discovered that the New Testament was the place she wanted to start. She found the four gospels, Matthew, Mark, Luke, and John and began to flip through.

Grace wasn't positive what she was looking for, so she just skimmed and turned pages. She grinned when she found the story of the good Samaritan. She stopped to read it, the first story she had ever read on her own from her own Bible. After she had finished reading that story, she went back to skimming. She felt quite satisfied once again when she came across the story of the prodigal son. She also read that whole story slowly and carefully. When she finished, she felt good about reading it, but she still had her questions.

Grace sat at her window once again. She was trying to put the questions she felt rolling around in her head into real words. What was really bothering her? She knew whatever the problem was, it had something to do with this week's challenge.

"Okay, what exactly is the challenge," Grace thought to herself as she tried to sort things out. "Mr. Fuller said to clear the decks and take our sins to the Lord. Okay, what does that mean? He said we might have to apologize to someone and ask her or him to forgive us. Okay, maybe I have done something stupid to someone, and I need to tell them I'm sorry."

Grace's thoughts were interrupted by what sounded like a small freight train banging its way down the hall. She shook her head in frustration and disbelief as she heard Ryan careen off her bedroom wall, nearly knocking down a picture. This was followed by a clear thud at the end of the hall as Ryan fell flat, on his face she hoped. All of this was accompanied by Avis yapping.

Grace flew to her door and wrenched it open ready to yell and scream. He had interrupted her again. He was keeping her from understanding things she really wanted to figure out. He was driving her crazy! She stepped out into the hall, and she could see Ryan flinch as he got ready for whatever she was going to do. Even as Grace opened her mouth to yell, she realized that here was a person she really owed an apology. Grace was as surprised as Ryan was by what came out of her mouth.

"Hey, Ryan, I need to tell you something."

"Yeah, I know. Stop running. Stop playing. Stop bothering you. Stop doing anything that's fun," Ryan just got the list started for her.

"Well, not this time bro. I just wanted to tell you I'm sorry for all the times I've yelled at you for no reason, or I haven't helped you when I could have. I will try harder to be a better big sister. I hope you'll forgive me," Grace was enjoying the stunned look on Ryan's face. She was also enjoying how good this was making her feel inside.

Ryan was trying to find the catch, "That's what you wanted to come out here and say? No yelling or screaming?"

"That's it—this time."

Ryan grinned, "Alright then. Sure I forgive you. I guess I'll try to be a better little brother too."

With that, Ryan was up and bouncing off the walls into his bedroom. Grace shook her head and went back into her room, wondering where he got all his energy. Bev, on the other hand, still stood on the top step. The smile she wore was almost too big for her face. Had she just heard her kids saying they were going to try to be nicer to each other with no one threatening them? She dropped to her knees for a quick moment and thanked the Lord for her blessings.

Grace jumped at the soft knock on her door. Her mom walked in and smiled at her. Grace waited for her mom to freak or something when she saw the Bible lying on her bed. Grace was actually quite impressed when her mom managed to keep a straight face and both feet on the floor.

"How are things going Grace?" her mom asked as she sat down on the storage bench. She had seen the Bible but thought it might be better to approach things from a different direction.

"Oh, I think things are going pretty well," Grace wondered what her mom was up to with this little visit.

"Are you enjoying the youth group meetings up at church?" Bev tried to appear very interested in the stuffed cat on the bench beside her.

"They've actually been really great," Grace decided to give her mom a break and tell the truth.

"I'm glad to hear that," Bev had to fight the urge to dance a little jig. "Have you talked about anything you want to discuss? Do you have any questions about anything I might be able to help you with?"

Once again Grace was impressed with her mom's self control, "So far I've really liked what we've talked about, and the weekly challenges are really fun."

"Good, what are weekly challenges?"

Grace groaned inside. She felt like she had said too much, "Oh, just little things that Mr. Fuller asks us to try to do during the week."

Bev noticed the vagueness was returning, so she rose to leave, "I'm glad you're enjoying the meetings. If you ever have any questions about anything, you can come to me, or, if you'd rather, just let me know and I'll try to find someone else who might be able to help."

Bev left the room feeling good about things. She felt her prayers were being answered. She certainly would have liked a speedier resolution to Grace's problems, but that was not her call. She was learning to lean on God and place her trust in Him. She hoped Grace was learning this too. She allowed herself a silent scream of happiness as she skipped down the hall.

Grace stared after her mom. She wondered when she had learned to stay so calm. Grace knew her mom had to have wanted to ask about the Bible being out on the bed, but she didn't. She also knew her mom had to have wanted to ask for specifics about the weekly challenges, but she didn't. Grace hoped that some day she would learn what had caused this change in her mom. Grace still felt like she had things to figure out, but she decided she had no more thinking in her today, so she went to do her homework.

During band class the next day, Jennifer began telling Grace about the person she was planning on apologizing to that night. It was a girl from her old school in Oklahoma. Grace was surprised Jennifer was digging so deeply for someone to say sorry to. Grace was almost embarrassed to tell Jennifer that she had only apologized to her little brother, but Jennifer thought it was great.

"Wow, I'll bet it was tough to say that to your brother. I'm quite impressed!"

Jennifer's reaction made Grace feel much better, "It really wasn't as hard as I thought it would be. I'm still thinking about things though. I think there may be other people that need to forgive me for doing something stupid. Have you thought about apologizing to more than one person?"

"Oh sure. I've certainly done more than one stupid thing to more than one person. I doubt I can get all the apologizing done in one week that I need to do!" Jennifer said with a laugh, "I'm just lucky God will forgive me for all those stupid things!"

Grace laughed with Jennifer although she doubted Jennifer had done one mean thing in her entire life. She also thought

Jennifer had just helped her figure out one of the biggest questions she had been trying to put into words. She looked carefully at Jennifer, but decided she needed to do some thinking before she just blurted it out in the middle of band class.

That evening Grace sat where she usually did her thinking. She really didn't have a great view from the window in her room, just the house across the street, but it was a quiet place for her to ponder things. Tonight she was mulling over a big question. It had been on her mind since she had talked with Jennifer that morning.

"Why would God forgive me?" she wondered, "I can't think of anything I've ever done to deserve to be forgiven. I know Mr. Fuller said all I have to do is ask and God will forgive me, but I don't understand why He would do that. I do stupid things all the time, and I'm sure I won't stop doing stupid things even after I apologize to people for the stupid things I've already done. Why would God waste time with me?"

Grace considered flipping through the Bible some more. Maybe she could find something that would explain things. She looked at the book that was now lying on her nightstand. As much as she wanted to learn the answer to her question, she decided it would be a waste of time for her to skim through any more pages not knowing where to start. That left her wondering how she was ever going to learn the answer.

Even as these thoughts were rolling around in Grace's head, she realized she still had someone she really needed to tell she was sorry. She had been avoiding thinking about this, but the name kept popping into her head every time she turned around. She wanted to shake her head until the name fell out, but figured the name would just turn up somewhere else. She was going to have to face Rebecca.

Grace found that as soon as she decided she was going to apologize to Rebecca, she already felt a little better. Now the big problem—what was she going to say? How was she going to face her after all the terrible things she had said that day at lunch? Why would Rebecca ever forgive her anyway? Grace didn't think she would ever forgive anyone she over heard talking about her the way she had been talking about Rebecca. Why had she done that in the first place?

"Another good question," Grace mused. "Rebecca's always been nice to me. Why would I do that to her?"

Of course, Grace wouldn't have said any of those things if she'd known Rebecca was listening. Grace then thought about how she had felt when she had walked by the table in the cafeteria and heard those kids talking about her. They hadn't known she was going to walk by them either. Their not meaning for her to hear hadn't kept her from feeling awful. Not meaning for Rebecca to hear was not an excuse. She was going to have to come up with a good apology for this one.

GRACE SPENT THE NEXT COUPLE OF DAYS TRYING TO figure out what she was going to say to Rebecca. Every time she saw her, she wanted to apologize, but she ran the other way. It was now Friday, and Grace knew it was time to get this over with no matter what Rebecca's reaction might be. She walked into English class determined that she was not going to chicken out this time. She was too late to talk to Rebecca before class, so she decided when the bell rang it was time to ask for forgiveness.

It was difficult to pay attention during class, as Grace waited for the bell to ring. When it finally did ring, Grace felt her breathing and heart rate speed up, and she could barely swallow. She was not going to run away. She attempted to take a deep breath, and walked up to Rebecca.

"Could I talk to you a minute, Rebecca?" Grace asked quietly. When Rebecca just looked at her, Grace went on quickly, "I wouldn't blame you if you told me to go away, but I was hoping you would give me just a minute. You don't even have to say anything."

As if sensing how much Grace was suffering, Rebecca said fairly nicely, "Alright, go on."

"Thanks," Grace breathed a small sigh. At least Rebecca wasn't going to just walk away. Now, if she could just remember what she wanted to say, "I, uh, I just wanted to apologize to you for what I said in the lunch room the other day. I have no excuses. I really don't even know why I said it. I've always liked you and enjoyed talking with you and working on things with you. I can't imagine why you would, but I was wondering if, maybe, you might, uh, forgive me. Some day maybe? I mean, hopefully you can, some day."

Grace could barely breathe. She hadn't said exactly what she had practiced. Things always seemed a little harder in real life. She hoped she'd done well enough to convince Rebecca how truly sorry she was. She waited anxiously for Rebecca to say something.

Rebecca seemed to pause to think a moment. She looked Grace right in the eye as she answered, "I do believe you're sorry, Grace," Rebecca paused. Grace felt hopeful, "I'm just not sure I believe you when you say you don't know why you said those things. I have always thought of you as a friend. I know we've never spent a lot of time together, but we've talked a lot and we've done projects together. I would never have expected you to talk about me behind my back, especially not in such a mean way. I am working on forgiving you. I've been praying about it, and I think you apologizing will help a lot."

Grace wasn't sure how she was feeling. Events weren't unfolding as she had hoped. Rebecca still hadn't said she had forgiven her. Grace really wasn't sure what Rebecca had meant by the things she had said. She stood and waited to see what would happen next.

After a minute, Rebecca took a deep breath and went on, "Grace, I know saying this to me had to be really hard. I have no idea how hard. But … I still feel like you have some thinking to do. You really should know why you said those things. I think you do know why, but you don't want to believe it or something. I guess I want to say that I think you did a great thing by apologizing. I plan to forgive you, but you're going to have to give me a little time. I think you should really try to figure out why you did this to me. Maybe things will make more sense to both of us when you figure out what's really happening."

"Thanks Rebecca," Grace whispered as Rebecca headed off to lunch. Grace turned to follow. She couldn't quite decide how she was feeling, but she knew she'd done the right thing.

Grace didn't feel like smiling and laughing at lunch. She prepared herself for questions just in case someone had seen her talking to Rebecca. She wasn't about to make the same mistake twice, but she wasn't sure what she would say. She didn't have to worry about it, as Hope could only talk about some new guy in her science class, who was amazingly cute and nice. Grace was relieved and smiled and nodded as she let her mind wander.

She was rather proud of herself for going through with her apology to Rebecca. It had taken a lot of courage for her to do that. She was glad Rebecca seemed to understand how hard it had been for her to talk about what happened. She didn't understand why everyone was so caught up with why she had said what she had. Jennifer had asked her why she had done it too. Well, she had more thinking to do when she got home this afternoon. She hoped her brain didn't explode from all the thinking she was doing these days.

As Grace sat in her usual after school spot in her room, she found she just couldn't make sense of her jumbled thoughts. She decided what she needed was someone to talk things over with. Maybe if she could say things out loud they would start to make a little more sense. Okay, now that she made that decision, she had to decide who that someone would be.

The first person Grace thought of to talk to was Christina. How she missed their talks. As much as she would have loved to talk to Christina, somehow Grace just didn't feel Christina would understand what she was going through right now. She didn't know what Christina might say or do if she brought up God and forgiveness. She decided she would have to think of somebody else.

Grace knew her mom would love to listen. She would also probably have some useful ideas and might even understand more than Grace did at this point. But she was still Mom, and she would probably be shocked at some of the things that had happened, especially with Rebecca. She was a possibility, but Grace thought there might be someone else she'd rather talk to.

Jennifer was the person Grace thought might understand and be able to help her. Jennifer already knew about the "Rebecca incident", and she already knew about the challenges from youth group. Grace felt Jennifer had a much better understanding of faith and forgiveness and stuff than she did. Maybe Jennifer could even help her figure out why she hadn't felt truly happy in such a long time.

Grace had made her decision. Now she just had to act on it. She was impressed with the way she had been making decisions and following through on them. She hoped she didn't let herself down now.

Since Grace had decided face to face was going to be the best way to talk to Jennifer, she went to her mom and asked if Jennifer could come over for a while Saturday afternoon. She decided she didn't want to go anywhere and home seemed like a safe place to have this little meeting. Grace wasn't quite prepared for her mom's reaction to what she considered a rather run of the mill request.

"Jennifer! Sure! Sure, she's welcome anytime. Why don't you go ahead and call her now. I hope she's home. This is a little bit on the short notice side," Bev tried to control her excitement but could tell by the baffled look on Grace's face that she wasn't doing a very good job.

"Okay, mom. It will only be for a little while in the afternoon," Grace wondered what the big deal was.

"Sure, she can stay as long as you like," Bev had been hoping Grace and Jennifer would become better friends. Maybe things were working out at last.

Grace called Jennifer. Jennifer sounded happy about the invitation, and her mom gave the okay. Grace had set things in motion, and there was no backing out now. She hoped this worked.

Grace had managed to make herself quite nervous by the time Jennifer arrived the next day. What had she done? She couldn't help but wonder if she'd made a huge mistake. She hated not knowing how things were going to work out!

Jennifer finally arrived. She said hello to Grace's mom, and then the two girls went upstairs to Grace's room. They sat around and talked about band class for a while, laughing about how badly everyone was doing on the piece of music they were trying to learn. As they stopped laughing, Grace tried to lead the conversation in another direction.

"How did you do with this week's challenge?"

"Well, I called my friend from Oklahoma and asked her to forgive me. She actually laughed! She had forgotten about the time I ignored her in class and didn't help with her paper," Jennifer laughed, "So that worked out. I also apologized to everyone in my family. I feel pretty confident my "decks are clear," at least of everything I can remember! How about you?"

"Well, I told my little brother I was sorry for the way I've been treating him lately," Grace began, "and I talked to Rebecca yesterday."

"Wow, she didn't tell me. How did that go?"

"Uh, well, it went. She said she needed some time."

Jennifer nodded, "I can understand that. I hope you can too."

"Oh, I can. She was nicer to me than I probably would

have been to her," Grace said quickly, "She also said she thinks I need to figure out why I said those things about her."

"Yeah, I can understand that too," Jennifer nodded again.

"Me too. Well, kind of anyway," Grace was so confused about things she didn't even know where to start.

Jennifer seemed to sense there was something else Grace wanted to say, "Do you have any ideas about why you said those things? As I get to know you better, I know I don't understand. You don't seem to be that kind of person."

Grace looked at Jennifer, "I never have been. I'm having trouble figuring things out right now."

"What kinds of things are bothering you?" Jennifer looked concerned, not judgmental as Grace had feared.

"Well, I don't really know where to start."

"Start wherever you want," Jennifer sounded like a friend.

Grace took the leap. She started back at the beginning with the first day of school. She told Jennifer about Christina and how their friendship had changed. She mentioned Hope and how she never knew what she was thinking. She even told her about how she felt she could actually be kicked out of "the group", and how she'd never felt that way with friends before. After saying all that without stopping to take a breath, she paused to look at Jennifer.

Jennifer was just listening. She would nod and say "oh" or "ouch" or whatever was appropriate at the time. Grace could tell she was really listening, so she went on with her story. She told her about her decision to fit in with "the group" no matter what because she had to find a way to make herself happy. She even told her about how hard she was finding it to sit at the lunch table with them, especially when she was tired.

Grace threw herself back on the bed. She hadn't really planned on sharing quite so much. She had to admit, though, it felt good to talk about all this stuff. She sighed and looked up at Jennifer.

"Am I pathetic?"

Jennifer laughed, "Hardly! I didn't realize everything you are dealing with this year. I hope I haven't been making anything harder for you."

It was Grace's turn to laugh, "You being in band has been the best thing that's happened this year."

"Well, considering how miserable you are, that's not saying much!"

The girls laughed until their stomachs hurt. Bev happened to walk by the door and hear them. She smiled and hummed on her way down the stairs, thinking that God is good.

After finally calming down, Jennifer looked at Grace and asked her, "What are you planning to do next?"

"That's always the question. I'm always trying to decide what to do next," Grace was unsure even where this conversation was going to go next.

Jennifer looked sympathetic. "It does always seem one thing just leads to another thing that leads to another question."

"I haven't even told you the whole story about apologizing to Rebecca yet."

"All right, I'm ready. How did you ever go through with that?" Jennifer was impressed.

Grace told Jennifer the whole story this time. She told her word for word what she had said and what Rebecca had said. She even told her how she had felt through the whole thing, and it was hard to put that into words. When she finished, she waited to see what Jennifer would say.

"Well, you had told me she said she needed time. I know that must still be hard, but do you understand why she wants you to figure out why you said the things you said?"

"I do and I don't," Grace said honestly, "I guess I would want to know if someone was mad at me or something and that's why they said mean things about me. I wasn't mad at Rebecca."

"No, I didn't think so. You mentioned that you and Rebecca talked before lunch that day. Tell me exactly what happened then."

"Okay. Let's see. We were standing out in the hall talking about something that happened in class, I don't remember what. We were laughing. We both were supposed to go to lunch next, so we weren't in any hurry. Lots of people were walking by us, probably wondering why we were just standing there. Oh, Hope and Christina were two of the people who walked by while Rebecca and I were laughing."

Jennifer asked, "Did they say anything?"

"No, they barely even looked at us. I didn't really give it much thought until I sat down to eat and they started to bother me about why I was talking to her," Grace paused and looked at her hands.

"Did you just figure out something?" Jennifer asked softly.

"Maybe I started saying those mean things about Rebecca to get them to leave me alone. They just kept making fun of me for talking to her," Grace was not happy with the words that were coming out of her mouth. "I don't know why I would have done that! I made fun of Rebecca because they were making fun of me, and I wanted them to stop! I started saying mean things about her, and they started laughing and left me alone. What kind of person does that?"

"A normal person who's been backed into a corner."

"Well, I don't want to be normal then!"

Jennifer took a deep breath and continued carefully, "None of us wants to make those kinds of mistakes, but most of us make them all the time. That's why we have to apologize to so many people so often."

"And what good does that do? They don't believe us, and then we just go out and make the same mistakes again."

"Yeah, we do that a lot it seems," Jennifer agreed, "but I think, or hope, that eventually we learn from our mistakes. Then we can apologize, ask God for forgiveness, and start trying to be better people. Sounds so simple doesn't it?"

"Sure, it sounds that way," Grace saw the opening for her question, so she took a deep breath and dove in, "Why would God want to forgive me? Rebecca can't forgive me. Why should God?"

"Now there's a tough question. I also think it's really important that we get the right answer to this question," Jennifer spoke slowly, choosing her words carefully, "We may have to get some help on this one."

"Yeah, I've been trying to come up with someone who could help me, but there's always some reason not to ask them," Grace was a little disappointed that Jennifer didn't want to, or couldn't, just answer the question herself.

"Okay then, we'll come up with some way to ask someone who could give us a good answer without actually asking them!"

Grace could tell Jennifer had an idea, "Okay, sounds a little complicated but let's hear it. What's the plan?"

"Well, I was thinking that tomorrow morning at church…"

The girls talked and planned for the rest of the afternoon. By the time Jennifer went home, Grace was feeling pretty good about what they were going to do. It was just a little sneaky, but it wasn't going to hurt anybody. Grace was thinking it just might help a bunch of people. She and Jennifer had decided that if they wanted to know the answer to this question, then there were probably others who wanted to know too, even if they hadn't been able to put it into words yet. Grace was actually looking forward to church the next day.

six

GRACE WAS IN
the living room the next morning holler-
ing for the rest of the family. Bev couldn't
remember the last time that Grace was the
first one ready to go anywhere. She also
couldn't remember Grace ever being in a
hurry to get to church. She knew something was going on, and she just hoped it
was something good.

As soon as Grace walked in the door
of the church, she started looking around
for Jennifer. She almost screamed when
she saw her walking towards her. The
girls were smiling and whispering as they

slowly wandered away from their families and around the corner.

"Do you have it?" Jennifer whispered as she choked on giggles.

"Of course!" Grace pulled out a sheet of paper and handed it to Jennifer.

"Oh no! You keep it. I'm the distraction, remember?"

"Got it!"

The girls crept down the hall toward the church office. They tried to act natural, but the fits of laughter threatened to blow their whole plan. They stopped in front of the office and took some deep breaths. Then Grace reached out and turned the knob. As they were about to go inside, Mr. Fuller walked by and waved.

"Hi, girls. How are you two doing this morning?"

Grace pulled her hand away from the knob like she'd been burned, "Oh, we're good Mr. Fuller. We're fine."

"Great," he smiled at them, "I hope to see you both tonight."

"Oh, we'll be there. We wouldn't miss it," Jennifer said with a crazy smile on her face.

"I'll see you then," Mr. Fuller walked away.

Jennifer and Grace looked at each other as he turned the corner and then raced into the bathroom where they almost fell on the floor laughing. They tried to calm down when an elderly woman walked in, but it was no use. The woman eyed them suspiciously and walked back out. The girls decided they were just going to have to laugh until they were finished laughing.

Grace looked at Jennifer as she wiped the tears from her eyes, "Are you ready to try again?"

Jennifer tried desperately to keep a straight face as she answered, "Sure!"

As soon as the word was out of her mouth, she dissolved into laughter again. Grace tried to look stern, but that only made Jennifer laugh harder. Once Grace gave up and started laughing too, it took them another five minutes before they even tried to leave the bathroom.

When they finally emerged, the girls found that no distraction was going to be necessary for them to accomplish their plan. They had laughed for so long that the service had started. Everyone was already in the sanctuary, and the church office was empty. All the girls had to do was walk in and stick the piece of paper into Mr. Fuller's mailbox. They folded the paper in a strange way so that it would kind of stick up and be very noticeable. As soon as their mission was accomplished, they ran out of the office and into the already-in-progress worship service.

As Grace slipped into the pew next to her mom, she could tell her mom was a bit annoyed with her. She had given her quite a look. Grace just shrugged her shoulders and tried not to laugh. She turned around and looked at Jennifer and saw that she, too, was trying not to burst. Grace turned around quickly and stared straight ahead for the rest of the service. She couldn't risk looking back at Jennifer again. She wasn't sure just how her mom would react if she were to fall out of the pew laughing during the morning prayer. She couldn't wait to see what would happen at the youth group meeting later that night.

Bev wondered what Grace and Jennifer had been up to before church started. She was not happy that Grace had come into the service late, but she was happy to see Grace laughing. She seemed happier on the weekends when she got the chance to spend more time with Jennifer. Bev had talked with Jennifer's mother Marie who said the same thing about Jennifer. Bev hoped this would develop into a true friendship, something she wasn't sure Grace had right now.

Grace and Jennifer said a quick good-bye after church. They were both on the verge of laughter, so they thought it best just to get out of there and see each other later at the meeting. Grace was sure Jennifer was just as excited as she was to see how Mr. Fuller was going to react to the message they had left for him. Maybe her search for an answer was almost over.

Grace tried to do her homework that afternoon, but spent most of her time pacing around her room. Her active imagination just wouldn't stop trying to come up with different scenarios for the upcoming meeting. Would Mr. Fuller just ignore the message? Would he be mad? Would anyone really be interested in what she and Jennifer were trying to understand? Grace groaned out loud and forced herself to sit and finish her math.

Grace was impatient waiting for the youth group meeting that evening. She ended up arriving a few minutes early. As she walked quietly into the room where they met, she saw Jennifer already sitting in her usual spot near the front. Grace crept up behind her.

"Boo!" she said.

"Oh, uh! Hi!" said Jennifer a bit startled.

"It seems we are both early," Grace said as she sat down next to Jennifer.

"It seems that way," Jennifer was grinning at her now.

"What do you think is going to happen?" Grace asked in a whisper.

"I don't know. Hopefully we're about to learn something really cool about God," Jennifer whispered back.

Grace was always surprised at how positive Jennifer could be, and also how she could talk about God as if he were right there in the room with her. She never seemed to worry about anyone else listening. Grace was hoping to have faith like that some day, faith she wouldn't be embarrassed to share with everyone she met. She also hoped she'd be taking her first step toward that kind of faith tonight. At the very least, it was going to be interesting to see what Mr. Fuller had to say.

Slowly the youth of the church trickled into the room. By starting time, there were sixteen people chatting and laughing. It was an average crowd for a Sunday night meeting, though the group was growing. One week they even broke the twenty mark. Mr. Fuller had been excited but nervous about that. He told everyone he was dedicated to the growth of the youth group, but he was worried because volunteers to help with their group were often hard to come by.

Everyone got quiet as Mr. Fuller entered the room. He laid some stuff on a table and turned around to face the students with a smile on his face. Grace and Jennifer exchanged a glance and anxiously waited to see what was going to happen.

Mr. Fuller started the meeting in his usual way. He greeted everyone and asked if there were any first time visitors. Since there was no one there for the first time, he pulled up a chair and looked around at the group in front of him with his eyes dancing. He looked to Grace like he was holding back laughter.

"Well, I have to say that something happened today that hasn't happened to me in the four years I've been working with this group," he seemed to watch each student as he spoke, "I received some "special" mail today in my church mail box. I don't know who it's from, so no one has to worry that their cover has been blown."

As he spoke, Grace and Jennifer fought to keep breathing evenly, and they didn't dare look at each other. Experience had already taught them what would happen if they did that.

"This, uh, letter, we'll call it, was different from any letter I've ever received," as he continued talking, Mr. Fuller pulled a sheet of paper from his pocket. Grace and Jennifer sucked in a breath as they recognized the paper. "This is what I found this morning."

Mr. Fuller held up the paper and turned it so everyone could see it. It was a regular piece of notebook paper. What made this letter unique had all of the students at the meeting whispering to each other. As Mr. Fuller turned the paper over, everyone could see that the message was written using words cut out of magazines. Some of the youth started asking questions.

"What does it say?"

"Alright, who sent the letter?"

"What are you going to do with it?"

"Who would send a letter like that?"

Mr. Fuller tried to cut in, "Ok, ok, if you'll get quiet I'll read you the letter."

It took a bit for everyone to settle down. Grace and Jennifer tried to act surprised like the other youth. They looked at each other and asked the same questions the others were asking, even as they tried to hide their smiles. As their leader tried to get everyone's attention, the girls found they couldn't look at each other anymore. The danger of laughter was present yet again.

When it was finally quiet enough, Mr. Fuller began to read the glued together letter, "It says: Mr. Fuller, we have questions. We are not sure how to ask them. We do not want to ask them in front of the whole group. Maybe you could think of a way for us to ask questions anonymously. This is our first question. Why should God forgive us? We don't think we deserve it."

There had been some snickering in the room until the question had been read. Then silence fell over the room. Everyone seemed to look down at his or her hands and then back up at Mr. Fuller. Everyone seemed to be waiting for the answer.

Mr. Fuller took a moment to clear his throat, and then he continued, "First, I want to say I've spent most of the day driving my wife nuts by talking about ways you guys can ask me questions anonymously." There was some giggling. "I know, but I think I finally came up with an idea."

Mr. Fuller reached around behind the table in front of the room. He pulled out a box. It looked something like the Valentine boxes Grace had made in grade school for parties. It was covered with colorful wrapping paper and had a slit in the top for papers. There was more laughter from the youth as Mr. Fuller placed the box on the table.

"Is it Valentine's Day?" someone called out.

"Oh, I know what it looks like," Mr. Fuller said with a

grin, "but you've got to give me a break. I only had since after church this morning to come up with this idea and to make it workable. Anyway, this is our new question box. If you have any questions that you don't want to ask in front of the group, you can just write them down on a slip of paper and slide them into this box. I don't think you need to go to the trouble this person went to," he waved around the letter he'd gotten that morning, "I am not the kind of person to try to match up handwriting or notice ink color or anything like that. I believe you will be safe if you just write down your question in your own handwriting. So, what do you think of the question box?"

The youth began to applaud. Grace and Jennifer gave each other a satisfied grin. They were thrilled Mr. Fuller had taken their letter so seriously. They knew their method of writing had been a bit over the top, but it had been fun. They also knew no one would ever know it had come from them.

"Alright then," Mr. Fuller said, "I'll put the box right by the door to this room. You should be able to just walk by and drop in a paper without drawing any attention to yourself."

Mr. Fuller cleared his throat again, "Now, for the question. Why should God forgive me? This is a question nearly everyone asks at one time or another, and sometimes we ask it even after we know the answer. We know we are all sinners. Mistakes abound in all of our lives. We often do what we want, when we want, how we want. When we do this, we are often not even thinking about what God would want us to be doing, or how He would want us to do it. We hurt people. We are selfish. We don't think before we act. We generally are just a big mess!"

As he paused, Grace glanced around a bit and saw many of the people around her nodding. Everyone appeared to be listening intently. Grace felt a warmth in her heart she wasn't accustomed to. She could not describe the feelings she was experiencing. She practically held her breath as Mr. Fuller continued talking.

"God knows we're not perfect. He made us! He knows us better than we know ourselves. God allows us to make choices. He didn't want a bunch of mindless robots doing what He told them. God wants us to choose to follow Him. He knows we're still going to make mistakes. The difference is that once we have decided we're going to live for God and we invite Him into our hearts, then we try our very best to live right. We try our very best to listen to God and to do His will. But you know what? We are still going to make mistakes! We are still going to be human! We are still going to stumble along the way! So have you heard anything yet that makes you think there's something you can do to deserve to be forgiven by God?"

Grace was confused. Mr. Fuller still hadn't said anything about what she could do to deserve forgiveness. She was beginning to wonder if he was ever going to get around to giving her some directions. She needed someone to tell her what to do. She needed someone to get her on the right path. How was she ever going to figure this out on her own? Grace could feel herself starting to get panicky.

Jennifer seemed to sense that Grace was letting her imagination run wild again as she leaned over and said, "I think we're about to get to the good part."

"I sure hope so," Grace whispered back.

Since no one was really answering, Mr. Fuller plunged back into his speech, "Why should God forgive me? Well, technically, if it all depended on me, I would never be forgiven. There's always some temptation I can't resist. There's always some stupid thing I'm going to do. Lucky for me, and for everyone, God will forgive me whenever I ask. I don't have to beg and plead and then hope. I don't have sit around and wonder what I should be doing to make sure God has forgiven me. All I have to do is be sorry for what I did. That's right; I just need to be sorry. Sometimes I need to say I'm sorry. Like the challenge I gave you for this week, we sometimes need to go out and say sorry to others. Those you apologize to may or may not forgive you, but God always forgives you. God forgives you because He loves you. It sounds easy I know, but God doesn't ask us to jump through hoops. He just asks us to be sorry and to lay our burdens at His feet. He has made things easy for us."

Could it really be that easy? Grace found it a little hard to believe. She had heard Mr. Fuller say before that God made things easy for us, but she had still been trying to think of ways to punish herself and ways for God to punish her. Didn't she need to be punished?

"Shouldn't I get in trouble or something?" a guy down the row from Grace called out.

"Well, I'm not saying that if you do something stupid you're not going to get in trouble with your parents or that there may not be some sort of consequence you'll be facing. You know, if you jump without looking, you may just land on a cactus."

Grace barely heard the laughter as her mind was racing.

All she had to do was ask, and God would forgive her. She didn't have to promise to keep her room clean or never to be mean to her brother again. She could do this!

"Now," Mr. Fuller was talking again, "I would like to lead us in a very special prayer. If you haven't yet invited God into your heart and you feel ready for that, you will have the opportunity to do that. We will also ask God to forgive us for our sins so we can leave this room with a clean slate."

As she bowed her head, Grace was thinking of another time she had prayed for God to enter her heart. Just before she had been confirmed as a member of the church in sixth grade, the pastor had led them in a prayer like that. Grace had prayed along. She sat wondering if that prayer had "taken". Was God in her heart? She decided she would extend the invitation a second time just to be on the safe side. She smiled to herself as she also decided what her next question for the box would be.

Mr. Fuller led them in a lengthy prayer inviting God into their hearts and asking Him to forgive them of their sins. Grace thought it was the first prayer she had actually enjoyed. She felt that maybe her slate really was clean. Then her mind went immediately to wondering how long it would stay that way.

As Grace's mind tried to run off on another tangent, Mr. Fuller gave the youth their weekly challenge. "I had to change the challenge for this week since we had so many other things to talk about and didn't get to discuss our Bible story this evening. Don't worry; we'll get back on schedule next week. So here is your challenge for this week. I want you each to try to live each day this week the way you believe God would want you to live. We should try to do this all the time, but it's easy to get distracted. Try not to let the distractions get in your way this week. Try to keep your focus on God for the whole week. We'll talk about how things go next week. Don't forget to put any questions you have into the box. I'll check it each time I'm at church during the week. See you next week!"

Grace and Jennifer walked out together. Grace was trying to remember just exactly why she was trying to restrict their friendship. They said good bye as they each climbed into the cars where their moms were waiting. Grace knew they'd have a great time talking in band class the next day.

MONDAYS AND GRACE WERE NOT THE BEST OF FRIENDS. By the time she stopped hitting the snooze button, she barely had time to get ready. She had to grab a granola bar as she raced out the door to the waiting bus. She spent the bus ride nibbling and staring out the window. She thought there had to be a better way to get to school, that didn't involve a bus or her mom.

Grace had spent a little time the night before trying to think of ways she could live for God. She was a little confused on what she was supposed to do. She didn't think she could preach, and she didn't think she could change everything she did each day. She had finally decided she was just going to have to make decisions and choices as she met them. To her own surprise, she had prayed before going to sleep, asking God to help her make good choices this week. She stepped off the bus feeling determined to do things right for a change.

Grace felt like she had a pretty good morning. She didn't feel like she had done anything great, but she also didn't feel like she'd failed in her challenge yet. Maybe she didn't have to do anything great. Maybe she just had to do her best. Her mind wandered as she headed to the cafeteria.

Somehow, she made it through lunch, though Grace couldn't have told anyone what was discussed around the table. She darted from the table, excited to relax her smile and get to band class and talk to Jennifer. As she raced into the band room, she and Jennifer almost knocked each other down.

"I see you're in as big of a hurry as I am!" Jennifer laughed.

"Yeah, I wanted to talk to you. How are you doing with this week's challenge?" Grace asked.

"Well, I'm not sure really. I don't think I've done anything awful yet," Jennifer answered as she got her clarinet out of its case.

"That's pretty much how I'm feeling. I guess we'll know when we are facing something important," the girls had to stop talking as class began. Grace let her mind wander for a moment, and she wondered if she really would know when she was facing something important.

Grace arrived home in a fairly good mood. Bev was grateful for the change in Grace's attitude. It was wonderful to see her daughter happy. Bev knew things still weren't perfect for Grace, but she felt confident the tide was turning. She prayed it would keep turning in a positive direction. She could hear Grace and Ryan in the living room.

"Hey, Ryan," Grace was just saying hi as she passed through the room on her way up the stairs.

"Hey, Grace," Ryan looked up from the paper he was staring at. He didn't look happy.

Grace very much wanted to just keep walking, but, instead, she stopped, "What's wrong?"

"Math," Ryan's one word answer was filled with hopelessness.

"Math, always a challenge," Grace smiled at her own play on words as she decided to meet this challenge head on. "Maybe I could help you."

Ryan looked at her like she'd suddenly grown an extra head, "Help me?"

"Sure, I think I can manage a little third grade math. If you want the help, that is."

"Well, okay," Ryan handed her the paper.

Grace was a little surprised to see multiplication, but she dove on in. They worked together for a good twenty minutes. Grace felt confident Ryan understood what he was doing as she left him to finish on his own.

Bev could barely hold back the tears as she stood just out of sight and watched her daughter help her son with his homework. Under her breath she said a little prayer of thanksgiving. She could see her prayers being answered right before her eyes. She wanted to kick up her heels and sing a song, but she went to the kitchen to start supper instead.

After finishing her adventure with third grade math, Grace headed up to her room. She felt great. Wow, maybe she would be successful with this challenge after all. She decided she just had to call Jennifer.

"Wow, helping your little brother! Think maybe you're a saint?" Jennifer's reaction had Grace laughing.

"I seriously doubt that! But it did feel good. I think I was as shocked as Ryan was when I asked him if he needed any help. I think it was the right thing to do. I think I actually did what God wanted me to do!"

"You can't beat that! I'm hoping to feel like you do before the end of the week," Jennifer reinforced Grace's good feelings.

"See you tomorrow!" As she hung up the phone, Grace smiled and then got to work on her own homework.

The week went by quickly. Before Grace knew it, it was already Thursday afternoon. She was walking through the hall toward her locker when she saw Christina. She noted that Christina was alone, a pretty rare thing these days. Grace was a little surprised that her first reaction was wanting to turn a corner and run. She made herself walk straight up to Christina with a smile on her face.

"Hey, Christina. How's your day going?"

"Well, I'm glad there's only one hour left. Too many tests and quizzes for me. It's been a long week, don't ya think?" Christina began to dig around in the locker for her Spanish book.

"Actually, I think it's been a pretty good week. I'm looking forward to the weekend though," Grace tried to be honest. She felt this conversation was part of her challenge.

"Yeah, the weekend is always the best," Christina agreed, "Hope's got some great plans for all of us at the mall on Saturday. She's going to get her belly button pierced! You're coming aren't you?"

Grace supposed they had all talked about this at length at the lunch table, but it was news to her. She looked at Christina. She looked like the girl Grace had known for so long, but there was simply something different this year. "I can't imagine my mom letting me go to something like that, even if it's not me getting the piercing." The very idea of seeing such a piercing made her feel a bit sick.

"Well, I'm not going to tell my mom. You'll be missing something," Christina slammed the locker door and turned to go. "You should really think about coming."

Grace felt like Christina was being sincere in her invitation, but she also knew lying would not work. "I can't lie to my mom even if it's just by leaving out a few details, but I hope things go well for you."

Grace headed to class feeling like she had been successful in her challenge. She guessed she had probably left things out in the past when telling her mom where she was going and who she was going to be with, but it just didn't seem like a good idea any more. She wondered if Christina would really have fun on Saturday. Maybe it would be fun, but she was glad she was sticking to her challenge. For some reason Grace felt that even if God was okay with her watching someone get her belly button pierced, He wouldn't be okay with her lying so she could be there.

As it turned out, Grace ended up with other plans for Saturday. Jennifer called that evening and invited her over to her house for the afternoon. Grace's mom was supportive, so the plans were set. Grace was looking forward to the weekend even more now.

Friday was the slowest day of the week, as usual. Sometimes Monday was the worst, but it was usually Friday since it signaled free time ahead. It seemed that the more Grace looked forward to something, the longer it took for time to pass. She was looking forward to spending more time getting to know Jennifer. She liked how easy it was to laugh when they were together.

And laugh they did! All Saturday afternoon the girls talked and laughed. No subject seemed off limits. They talked about school, band, God, and B O I's. Jennifer thought the letters Hope had come up with for "boys of interest" were hilarious, so they made up letters for things the whole time they were at her house. They had their own M A S, a tough time figuring out T W A's, and laughed until their stomachs hurt when they talked about S O C's. Later on, they had to write down what the letters meant because they kept forgetting. They laughed even as they wrote down mid-afternoon snack, teachers with attitude, and siblings out of control.

The girls even got out their clarinets and played some duets. Grace had a great time and as she was getting ready to leave, she asked Jennifer if she felt she had succeeded in the weekly challenge. They both agreed the week had been a success. They had both worked to help their siblings. Jennifer had taken her cue from Grace and helped her little sister with her second grade spelling words. They both also tried to talk nicely with their parents and had been honest with people at school. But they also thought they needed a lot more work on keeping their focus on God. They said their good byes, looking forward to the next day.

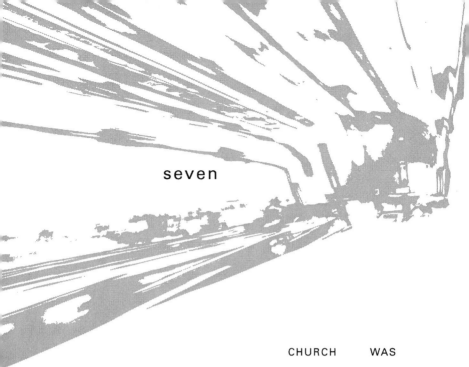

seven

CHURCH WAS fairly uneventful for Grace. She really tried to pay attention when the pastor spoke, but she had a hard time keeping her mind from taking another one of its trips. She felt she was taking steps in her faith, and she was really looking forward to the meeting that night. Each week, she felt she was learning more stuff she really needed to know to change her life. Maybe she would finally learn what she needed to know to make herself happy. She was beginning to see it as something she couldn't do on her own.

Grace and Jennifer were both early for the meeting again. They sat and whispered as the others arrived. After what seemed like ages, Mr. Fuller walked in to start the meeting. He said he was going to save the questions from the box until the next week. He explained that he was just seeing the questions for the first time that night, and he wanted a little time to look them over to prepare appropriate answers.

The story for the evening was about a woman named Ruth. Grace had heard of her before but wasn't sure what she had done. Apparently she had married the son of a woman named Naomi. Grace felt sorry for both of the women as the story went on to say that both women's husbands died. Naomi lost her other son as well. Grace couldn't see what she was going to learn from this, except that maybe her life wasn't really all that bad compared to what many others suffered.

As many of the youth were voicing her very thoughts, Mr. Fuller hurried to explain that the story was about loyalty and faith. The two women did not just sit down and despair, and Ruth did not abandon Naomi. Wherever Naomi went, Ruth went also. Mr. Fuller compared Ruth's loyalty to how God was always with them. He said the way Ruth followed her mother-in-law and did as she wanted her to is similar to how we should follow God and do His will.

Grace thought she would have just read the story and felt sorry for the losses of the two women. She figured she would have probably grown angry and bitter over the unfairness in her life if she had been the one in the story. She was impressed with how the women never gave up and how they depended on God. She wished she could depend on God like that. As

Grace returned to listening, she heard Mr. Fuller preparing to give them their weekly challenge.

"Okay, now for your challenge for the week. I want you to look for times when you can show your loyalty. You can do this with your friends, your family, and with God. Stand up for someone who can't stand up for him or herself. Help someone at home who didn't ask for help. Tell someone about something God has done for you whenever the opportunity presents itself."

Everyone started whispering and Mr. Fuller went on, "I know this may be hard. You may have to say things your friends won't like. But I know you can do it. You can go out there and show others how loyal you can be, how they can depend on you to do what's right. I'll see you next week!"

"Show loyalty?" Grace was confused. "How do you do that?"

"Well, I'm not sure," Jennifer sounded like she didn't really know either, "I think we may have another instance here where we just have to wait and find our answers when we meet the questions."

"Meet the questions? You're starting to sound more confusing than Mr. Fuller!" Grace was laughing.

The girls were still giggling as they called good bye and climbed into their cars. Bev looked at Grace.

"So I guess you had a good time tonight."

"Yes I did," Grace answered with enthusiasm.

"Well, I'm glad," Bev tried to sound nonchalant as she asked, "So, did you learn anything?"

"We talked about Ruth. I guess I didn't know much about

her," Grace was actually enjoying the conversation instead of getting upset about being interrogated.

"I don't think I know much about her either. Feel like enlightening me?"

Grace told her mom most of the story word for word as Mr. Fuller had presented it at the meeting. They talked and laughed all the way home. Grace didn't know how happy that made her mom. As soon as they pulled into the garage, Grace jumped out.

"Guess I better go get ready for another Monday."

"Maybe you could go to bed early, so you can get up in the morning," Bev suggested.

"We'll see," Grace was off up the stairs.

AFTER HER WEEKLY BATTLE WITH THE SNOOZE BUTTON, Grace made it up and to school on time. She was curious to find out what happened with Hope and the belly button piercing. She saw "the group" as soon as she entered the school building.

"Hey, Hope!" Grace called out when she saw them.

"Oh, hi Grace," Hope turned back around intending to keep walking in the other direction.

"Hey, Hope, did the belly button ring hurt?" Grace just had to find out what had happened.

Christina broke off from the group and walked over to Grace. "We're not supposed to talk about that."

"Oh, why not? Did it really hurt badly or something?"

"No. It didn't happen."

"Really," Grace was surprised, "what happened?"

"The guys working said she had to have her parents' permission. Her parents weren't there, so no piercing. Hope was really upset by the whole thing," Christina told the story with relish.

"Well, I guess, tell her I'm sorry she's disappointed," Grace said, secretly thinking that Hope may actually have been relieved things didn't work out as she had planned. Grace went on to her locker and prepared for the first class of the new week.

The week seemed to be going quite smoothly to Grace until Wednesday at lunchtime. Then Grace did something she never would have expected to do. She was walking through the cafeteria on her way to her usual spot. That was when she ran into Jennifer. Grace had never realized that Jennifer ate lunch at the same time she did. It seemed silly, she thought, that she wouldn't have known that.

"Hey, Grace!" Jennifer smiled.

"Hey, Jennifer," Grace wasn't sure what was going to happen.

"I was just getting ready to have a seat over there. Would you like to join us?"

Grace just looked at Jennifer. What was she going to do? She was torn. She always sat with Hope and Christina. What would they think if she sat somewhere else? Grace couldn't believe she was even considering sitting somewhere else after she'd worked so hard to earn the seat across from Hope. Yet, she was considering it. It sounded like fun. She always had fun with Jennifer, and she could smile without getting sore. What would it hurt just this one time?

"Sure, that'd be great!" she couldn't believe her own voice, but she couldn't wait to see how things would go.

"Great! Come on!" Jennifer seemed genuinely glad to have her come and sit with them.

As they reached the table, Grace felt her breathing speed up and she couldn't swallow any more. There sat Rebecca. What had she gotten herself into? Had Jennifer set her up?

"Hey, Rebecca! Grace is going to join us!" Jennifer looked at Rebecca as she spoke.

"Oh, okay," she looked up and gave Grace a small smile.

"If you'd rather I didn't… ." Grace started.

"Oh no, come on and sit down. I mean it," Rebecca's smile got bigger and Grace sat down.

Grace had a great time at lunch. The three girls were joined by a few other friends of Rebecca's, and they all had a great time together. Grace couldn't remember the last time she had laughed in such a "real" way at lunch. She and Jennifer walked to band class together.

"Thanks for inviting me to sit with you. I had a great time!" Grace told Jennifer as they walked.

"Anytime, and I mean that!" Jennifer laughed.

Later that afternoon, Grace ran into Christina at their locker. She was afraid of what Christina was going to say about her absence at lunch, but she bravely approached the locker.

"Hello Christina. How's it going?"

"Well, things are going pretty good today," Christina answered, "Although, as you heard, Hope is mad at Yvette. Isn't it driving you crazy that that's all Hope can talk about?"

"I'm not really around Hope that much during the day," Grace answered as casually as she could.

"Yeah, I know, but it would have been nice to talk about

something else for a while at lunch today, don't you think?" Christina was slamming the locker door as she looked at Grace for affirmation.

"Today at lunch?" Grace asked quietly.

"Of course today! Well, I've got to get going. See ya later, Grace!" Christina walked off down the hall, where she met up with Hope.

Grace watched after her. She felt a gnawing sensation in her stomach. Surely she was mistaken. She made lots of mistakes, so surely this was just another one. It almost sounded like—no, she couldn't even think it. She hung her head and leaned against the wall. She knew she should get moving, but her legs just didn't want to work yet.

A passing teacher looked at her, "Are you feeling alright?"

"Oh yes, yes, I'm okay," Grace answered. She finally got her feet to move, and she headed to seventh hour.

Grace was not in a good mood when she got home. She snarled at her mom, yelled at her brother, and even thought about hanging up on one of her mom's friends for calling when she wanted to use the phone. She finally just went up to her room and sat down by her window. She stared out, seeing nothing.

For a few minutes, all Grace could do was stare. She felt like her brain was numb. What had happened today? She had such a great day, and then it had been ruined in a few sentences exchanged in front of a locker. She shook her head as she willed her brain to make sense of everything.

Okay, she thought, I had a regular morning, a great lunch break, and then I talked to Christina. There was the problem. Grace had gotten somewhat used to her little exchanges with Christina by their locker between sixth and seventh hours. Exchanges was what Grace called their brief encounters because they didn't really have a conversation or anything, they just exchanged a few words. The exchange today had not been pleasant.

Christina had talked to Grace about the lunch conversation that had taken place at Hope's table. The problem was that she had talked to Grace as if Grace had been at the table! Today had been the first time all year Grace had sat somewhere else for lunch, and *no one had noticed!*

Grace could feel the tears welling up in her eyes. What was going on? How could the person she had always considered her best friend not even notice she hadn't been there? Grace wanted to get up and throw something, jump up down, stomp her feet, scream, and cry until her throat and eyes hurt, but she just sat there. She couldn't find the will to do anything but stare out the window as the tears slid slowly down her cheeks.

That was how Bev found her about twenty minutes later. She had knocked on Grace's door but had gotten no response, so she'd quietly walked in and looked around. She went over and sat beside Grace.

"Would you like to talk about whatever happened today?"

Grace looked at her with shining eyes, "I don't know. I don't know anything right now."

"Hmmm, I know that feeling. Maybe it would help if you just talked about it. I'd be happy to listen, or maybe you could call Jennifer," Bev suggested.

Grace realized she couldn't talk about this with Jennifer.

Maybe she could give her mom a chance. She took a deep breath and told her mom what had happened that day. She started with what happened at lunch and went through what happened in the hall with Christina. When she finished, she looked at her mom. She hadn't said anything yet, and Grace wondered what she was thinking and what she was going to say.

Bev was wondering the same thing. She wanted to be helpful but not sound like she knew everything. She certainly didn't want to say anything that would discourage Grace from talking to her again. She said a quick prayer for God to give her the right words, took a deep breath, and turned to Grace.

"Well, not such a great day in the end huh?"

"To say the least," Grace mumbled.

"I'm glad you talked to me. I have an idea how you feel, though I'm not going to tell you I know exactly how you feel. I've known things were not right between you and Christina since school started. I didn't know things had gotten like this. I am going to give you my opinion and you can do with it whatever you want, okay?"

Grace nodded, "Yeah, okay."

"Well, here are my thoughts. I believe you are trying very hard to be someone who you are not. Can you make sense of that?" Bev paused to see if Grace wanted to respond.

"Yeah, I guess so," Grace wasn't sure, but she thought once her mom said a little more, it might make more sense.

"Okay, well, I know you believe with all your heart that these girls you usually eat lunch with are your friends. If they are your true friends, then you should be happy to see them and happy to spend time with them. You need to ask yourself a few questions, in my opinion. Ask yourself what it is about these girls that you like. What about these girls makes you happy to be around them? Are these the people you run to when you have something to talk about? Do you feel included in activities? Do you really even like these girls?"

Grace was listening even as she stared out the window. She had been avoiding asking herself these very questions her mom was asking now. She knew the answers could be painful and confusing. She tried not to think about it too much right now and concentrated on what her mom was saying.

Bev could tell Grace was listening, so she decided to press on, "Do you feel like you're being yourself with these girls? It seemed to me that at the beginning of school you were not acting like yourself. I know things change, and you're growing into your own person. Believe it or not, I'm happy about that. I just want you to grow into a person you can like."

Grace turned to look at her for a moment. Bev was afraid that maybe she had said too much, but now that she had started, she really wanted Grace to know what she had been thinking for so long now.

Bev took in a breath and said, "I know you were not happy the first time I told you I'd pray for you. You thought I'd lost a few marbles or bumped my head one too many times. Well, I want you to know I'm still praying for you, everyday. I can see you are making strides in your life and in your faith. I'm hopeful you're happy now to know I'm praying for you, instead of being upset."

"I am," Grace whispered.

Bev felt close to tears but fought them back. "I can't tell you how glad I am to hear that. I don't have any definite answers for you. I believe you need to do some real, deep thinking and some praying. I think you can figure out where you're going to be the happiest. And, ya know, no one's happy all the time, but maybe you can figure out how to be at peace."

"I've been trying to make myself happy again since school started," Grace sounded hopeless.

"Maybe you should quit trying so hard to make yourself happy on your own and let God lead you to where you will be happy. I'm going to leave you to your thoughts unless you want me to stay," Bev was already thanking God for the privilege of being Grace's mom.

"I guess I better get busy thinking. Though I'm getting really tired," Grace tried unsuccessfully to muffle a yawn. She had decided this talking to her mom thing wasn't all that bad.

"Many problems take more than one evening to solve, Gracie. Rest will only help you to see things more clearly," Bev gave Grace a hug and a kiss and left as quietly as she had entered, grateful that Grace didn't react to her name slip up.

"Alone again," moaned Grace as she fell onto her bed and into a deep, troubled sleep.

eight

SOMEHOW GRACE

survived school on Thursday. She sat with "the group" for lunch and did her usual smiling. She thought she wasn't going to make it through. When the bell rang and released her from what she felt like was her torture, she ran to band. She was excited to get away from the lunch table, but she didn't really want to talk to Jennifer today. She didn't really want to talk to anyone. Her life was a mess and she didn't know how to fix it.

Jennifer seemed to sense her mood and kept the talking to a minimum. Grace appreciated it and also appreciated the encouraging smile Jennifer gave her as they parted ways after class. She was very glad Jennifer had moved into her band class and into her life that year.

Grace woke up the next morning and sighed. It was finally Friday! If she could just make it through one more day, maybe she could use the weekend to make sense of a few things. She got ready in record time and set off for the bus stop with a grim smile on her face.

Bev felt sorry for Grace but knew she had to find her own way. Grace knew she was available for talking or anything else she needed. She gave Grace what she hoped was an understanding and encouraging smile as she left for school.

Grace could have kicked herself as she stood in the lunch line. She had actually been ready early that morning, and she still forgot her lunch. If she hadn't been so hungry, she would have just said to forget it. But there she stood, waiting her turn for the Friday mystery special.

Grace was relieved when she finally got her tray and headed to her seat. She sat down heavily and prepared to dig into the small white mound on her tray she had been told was macaroni and cheese. She doubted the lunch lady's honesty as she took a bite, and then almost choked, not from the starchy substance in her mouth but from what she heard.

Hope was practicing her southern drawl again as she spoke. "Did y'all see that new gurl yesterdee?"

Christina was giggling, "Which "gurl" was that?"

"Oh, ya know. That one's in the band and hangs out wit dat Frankie gurl," Hope was laughing at her own bad accent.

Grace was frozen in mid bite. She knew exactly whom

Hope was talking about. She just hoped nothing awful was about to be said. She tried to chew the mass in her mouth as she listened to what came next.

"Oh yeah, I think her name is Jennifer," Christina glanced at Grace as she said the name.

"Yeah, that's the one. I think her nose is so far up in the air she's not been getting enough oxygen!" everyone was laughing, except for Grace, "She actually tried to talk to me this morning! She looked right at me and said 'Hi, how are you?' Just like I would want to answer her!"

"What did you do?" it was Yvette. Apparently she and Hope had made up. Grace wondered how long ago that had happened and she just hadn't been paying any attention.

"Well, I just looked at her and walked away! What am I supposed to do with a band geek like that? I have never seen a bigger geek in my whole life!" Hope thought this was hilarious.

Grace couldn't swallow the bite in her mouth. What was she going to do? She had never anticipated this. She had worked quite hard at keeping "the group" and Jennifer separate. Why were they doing this to her? She could hear the other girls talking and laughing. They were still talking about Jennifer.

Grace tried to let her mind wander so she wouldn't have to hear what they were saying. Her mind wandered straight to the Sunday night youth group meeting. It wandered straight to the story of Ruth and how loyal she had been to Naomi. Ruth had never knowingly let Naomi down. Grace knew what she had to do. She knew Jennifer would never let anyone talk about her like these girls were talking about Jennifer. This was her challenge, and it was a big one. She was going to have to face it whether she wanted to or not. She said a quick, silent prayer asking for the means to handle this challenge in the right way.

Grace looked around the table. These girls were not really mean people. She even liked some of them. She had seen several of them do nice things for other people, from holding doors to helping with projects. She didn't know why they felt they needed to talk about people the way they were right now. But, she guessed she really did know, since she had talked just like this more than once this school year. She was going to have to do some heavy thinking this weekend. She took the deepest breath she could take in and tried to prepare herself for what she was about to do.

Hope had just finished saying something about Jennifer's hair that Grace barely even heard when she opened her mouth to speak, "I know Jennifer. She's really nice and fun. You'd really like her if you got to know her."

"Oh really. Nice, is she?" Hope pretended to be fascinated.

"Yes, she is. She really doesn't deserve to be talked about like this," Grace could feel her cheeks getting red and knew she was dangerously close to stammering.

"Well, how does she deserve to be talked about?" Hope asked in an innocent voice.

The question caught Grace off guard. She had to take a minute before answering, but when she answered she meant every word she said, "She doesn't deserve to be talked about at all. No one does."

"Oh, I see," the bell rang before Hope could go any further.

Grace took her full tray up and put it away. She was just wondering how she was going to make it through the rest of the day, when she turned around and Jennifer was standing beside her.

"Shall we go to band?"

Grace smiled, "We shall!"

When Grace got home that afternoon, she was exhausted. She had decided not to make any plans for the weekend, so she could just spend some time thinking and figuring out what was happening in her life. She had never imagined that she, Grace Elizabeth Williams would find her friendships, plans, classes, everything in such a mess. Where had she gone wrong?

She threw herself down on the couch with a sigh and attacked the granola bar she had found in the kitchen. Ryan walked in and sat down beside her. He just sat and looked at her. Finally, Grace couldn't take it any longer.

"What are you looking at?" Grace kept her voice as even as she could.

"You. You don't seem very happy," Ryan kept looking at her as he talked.

"I'm not particularly jolly today," Grace tried to say it light-heartedly, but she knew she failed.

"I am still trying to be a better brother, so can I help you with anything?"

Ryan's sincerity almost brought tears to Grace's eyes, which she wasn't about to let happen, "No, but thanks. I think things will be better after the weekend."

"Ok, weekends are good for lots of stuff!" Ryan said and then ran off with Avis at his heels.

Well, even her little brother knew things weren't the way they should be. Maybe she really was the last person on the planet to figure out what a mess she was making of things. How had all of this happened? She was going to have to figure that out, and, while she was at it, she was going to have to figure out how to fix it.

As she was sitting slumped on the couch crunching away, the phone rang. Grace hopped up to get it, more out of habit then because she wanted to talk to anyone. She was surprised to hear Jennifer's voice.

"Hi, Grace. I was just calling to see if you wanted to go to the new movie theater that just opened by the mall tomorrow," Jennifer sounded excited.

Grace had wanted to go see a movie at the new theater for a few weeks. She had heard that the seats rocked and practically reclined and that each seat had its own cup holder and popcorn holder. Her plans to stay in and think went flying out the window.

"Wow, great! I'll go ask my mom!"

With her mom's permission, Grace made her plans. She and Jennifer were going to meet at the theater to see the cheaper afternoon show, and then they were going to walk over to the mall for a burger. She couldn't wait!

Grace tried to spend some time thinking the next morning. But by the time she finally got up, ate breakfast, and got ready to go, she didn't have much time to spare. She finally gave up and just let herself be excited about the movie. She had been a little surprised by Jennifer's invitation. So far, when they had gotten together, they had gone to her house or Jennifer's house. This was a new step for them. Grace hoped she wasn't making a mistake.

Grace and Jennifer walked out of the theatre laughing. The movie hadn't been very good, but the girls had laughed and giggled their way through it anyway. The seats had been just what Grace had expected, and she was having a great time. They made their way across the parking lot to the mall.

It took them about fifteen minutes to decide where they wanted to eat. They just kept saying, "Whatever you want to do" to each other. Finally, they just started laughing and went to the first place they had talked about.

They had a great time eating. It turned out they both loved curly fries and hated pickles on their cheeseburgers. Grace was glad she had come. This was the most fun she could remember having for a long time.

After they finished eating, the girls had thirty minutes left before Jennifer's mom was going to pick them up. They decided to walk around and window shop. They were laughing at some seriously underdressed mannequins when Grace saw Hope, Christina, Yvette, and a couple other girls round the corner down the hallway from them.

Grace suddenly felt panicked. What was she going to do? What would happen if "the group" saw her with the very person they had been making fun of just the day before? Grace tried to think fast. How could she avoid being seen without hurting Jennifer's feelings? She made a decision.

"Wanna go look around inside a minute?" she asked Jennifer as casually as she could.

"Well, I guess we could," Jennifer walked into the store.

Grace was relieved. She feigned interest in several racks of clothes until she saw Hope and "the group" pass by the store. Then she and Jennifer went on their way in the other direction. They had a great time until Mrs. Brown picked them up.

Back in her room by the window, Grace stared out at nothing once again. She was having guilt pangs from hiding in the store with Jennifer. How would she feel if someone didn't want to be seen with her? She already knew that answer and figured Jennifer would feel the same way.

What was she doing wrong? She had tried to make herself happy by trying to fit in with others. What was wrong with fitting in? Nothing, she decided, unless you simply were not the right shape for the puzzle.

She realized she had never really had fun with Hope. Mostly, she worked when Hope was around. She worked at smiling at the right time and in the right way. She worked at saying the right things at the right time and in the right way. She worked very hard at being what she believed Hope wanted her to be. Why was she doing this? She knew that answer too.

Everything she had done was because all of a sudden Christina had changed the rules of their friendship. They used to be so close, and then it had been "take Hope or lose me", or at least that's the way Grace had interpreted things. Christina had never really said those words. She had never told Grace she had to change herself to fit in. She had never told Grace to make fun of people or to ignore people or to be anyone other than herself. Grace had done that all on her own. It was time to take a little responsibility for her own actions.

Once she realized this, Grace felt ashamed of herself. She

had turned herself inside out to become someone she didn't even like! Why would anyone miss someone at the lunch table who just sat there pretending to be someone she wasn't? Wasn't she relieved when once in a while one of the other girls who she thought was trying too hard was absent? They probably felt the same way about her, and why shouldn't they?

Grace hung her head and felt the tears slide off onto her hands. She wasn't quite certain how to handle this hopeless feeling she had. What was she going to do? Could she keep sitting with "the group" if she really tried to just be herself? Would they even let her keep sitting with them? Would they like her as herself? What was she going to do?

The one highlight of the week, Grace thought, was she had succeeded in the weekly challenge. She had stood by Jennifer when the others had been making fun of her. She sat a little straighter in her chair by the window. She was proud of how she had handled that situation. She hoped she'd do the same thing if anything happened like that in the future. She also hoped she would never again be the one making fun of someone so mercilessly. She couldn't believe she had ever done that. Maybe she had finally learned that lesson at least.

Even as she was congratulating herself, her mind wandered back to earlier that evening at the mall. She hadn't exactly stood up for Jennifer there. She had hidden her. She hadn't wanted to be seen with her! She had run away from "the group" so they wouldn't see Jennifer. She had been afraid. Grace put her head in her hands. She wasn't much of a success after all.

Why had she done that? What was she really afraid of? Grace's head was starting to hurt. She stifled a yawn. Maybe she should sleep on it. After all, her mom had said many problems take more than one evening to solve, and these were big problems. Grace turned out the light and flopped onto the bed. Tomorrow was Sunday. Maybe she would learn something that would help her figure out some things. She rolled over and went to sleep.

BEV WOULD HAVE DESCRIBED GRACE AS A "BIG OLE hairy grouch" the next morning. Last Sunday, Bev remembered, Grace was ready to go to church, even eager. Today, she could barely seem to make herself move. She had come home from her outing with Jennifer in a strange mood. She said she'd had a good time, and Bev had believed her. Then she went upstairs and didn't come back down. When Bev finally went up to check on her, she was sprawled out on her bed asleep. Something was going on—again.

Grace was glad to get home from church. She found Ryan's enthusiasm and her dad's apathy hard to take today. She could tell her mom knew something was wrong, but she wasn't ready to talk about it yet. She kept herself busy all afternoon with homework and TV so she wouldn't have to think anymore. She had discovered she was not the person she wanted to be. She just didn't feel ready to learn about any more of her shortcomings.

Despite her mood, Grace was still a bit early for the youth group meeting that night. She ended up being the first person there. She went in and sat down in what had become her usual spot. She stared up at the cross that hung on the wall in the front of the room. She couldn't imagine the kind of courage it would take to allow someone to hammer a spike into your hands and feet and hang you up on a cross. She knew she didn't have that kind of courage. She wasn't even courageous enough to be seen with the nicest, kindest, most fun person she had been around for a long time. What a failure she was! She continued to stare at the cross. She found herself praying silently.

"Okay, God. I really don't know how to do this. I haven't prayed, really prayed, in a long time—maybe ever! Please help me find my way. Please help me to be the kind of person others want to be around. Please help me to understand … ummm, to understand the things I need to know. I want to be a better person," Grace heard others walking into the room so she quickly ended, "Amen."

"Hi, Grace. Is it ok if I sit down?" Jennifer seemed uncertain if she was interrupting something or not.

Grace mustered up a smile, "Of course! You better!"

"Great! I wasn't sure if you were doing something. You seemed deep in thought," Jennifer sat down with a thud.

"I guess it was pretty quiet in here, so my mind wandered," Grace tried to shrug off the question. "Here comes Mr. Fuller."

Grace and Jennifer turned to see Mr. Fuller walking in hurriedly. He always arrived at the last minute. It was kind of a running joke with the rest of the youth. He smiled as he threw his jacket in a chair and turned to face them.

Mr. Fuller got right down to business. He pulled out three slips of paper that had been in the question box. They were all questions about the story from last week. He answered them fairly quickly and asked for any other questions.

"If there are no other questions, we'll get right into the

story for tonight. We are going to discuss the story of Esther tonight."

There was a groan from the back row followed by, "Not another chick!"

"Yes!" Mr. Fuller smiled, "Another powerful, important woman! This one had a very rough childhood followed by a life as a queen."

Grace was intrigued. What could she learn from a woman who was a queen? She wasn't impressed with how she became queen. The king, Xerxes, got rid of his former queen, Vashti, because she didn't listen to him. They searched his kingdom for a new queen. Esther was one of the many girls brought in to meet the king. She was the lucky one the king liked, so she became queen. Grace knew she was simplifying things, but she was still wondering why Mr. Fuller had chosen this story for the meeting.

"Alright, I imagine some of you are wondering why I've chosen this story to discuss tonight," Grace almost snorted as she tried not to laugh, "but I'm getting to the good stuff, I promise."

As the story went on, Grace began to understand. Esther was made queen just a little while before the king's main guy, Haman, got really angry with Esther's Uncle Mordecai. Since Mordecai was a Jew, Haman decided to take out his anger on all of the Jews and not just Mordecai. Grace couldn't believe Haman got the king to sign a command saying that on a certain day people could kill all of the Jews and keep their belongings.

Mordecai sent a message to Esther, the queen and also his niece, asking her to talk to the king about the command.

Esther sent a message back to Mordecai reminding him that anyone who went to see the king without being summoned could be put to death if the king didn't raise his gold scepter to that person.

"So you see," Mr. Fuller was trying to explain, "things were going badly for the Jews, but, through events God had put in motion, Esther was in a position to help. The problem was Esther's fear. She was afraid to go before the king. She was afraid to tell him she was a Jew. Most of all, she was afraid he wouldn't raise his gold scepter to her, and she would die."

Now that, Grace decided, was something to be afraid of. Trying to help someone in a way that could get you killed was worthy of a little fear. Trying to help someone but not be seen by certain others, not so much. Once again Grace wondered what she should do next.

Well, Esther did go before the king and did eventually ask for his help. The king was very upset and the Jews were spared, but Haman was not. Mr. Fuller said Esther showed great faith by going before the king like that. She showed she trusted God to be with her even in a scary situation.

Grace was beginning to see how this story could relate to her own life. Did she trust God enough to do what she should do? Grace knew she was not in a life or death situation like Esther was, but it felt very scary to her none the less.

"Okay," Mr. Fuller was talking, "now for this week's challenge. I want you to try to do the right thing this week even when it is very difficult. When everyone is telling you to do this or that, but you know it's wrong—make a conscience choice to do the right thing. I know this can be very scary. I know this can be very difficult. But if you rely on God, and trust

Him to always be with you, even in a very scary, difficult situation, I believe you can do the right thing. See you next week! Remember we're meeting at the bowling alley next Sunday!"

Grace and Jennifer walked out of the meeting together as usual. Grace was having a hard time believing she could be successful with this new challenge.

"I don't think I'll be able to do the challenge this time," she said.

"Oh, I think it may be hard, but you can do it," Jennifer smiled at Grace.

"No, really. I've made a mess of a lot of things lately. I don't think I have it in me to do the right thing. Half the time, I don't even know what the right thing is anymore," Grace felt like a whiny little kid.

"Well, I'm not sure exactly what you're talking about. I think you're a great person. I know you've made some mistakes, but we all do that. I've also seen you make up for those mistakes. It takes a very courageous person to walk up to someone they've hurt and apologize," Jennifer was very sincere.

"You're always so nice. Why can't I always be nice? No, I have to be the one who has to somehow apologize for all the rotten things I do," there was that whining again, but it felt good to talk about it.

"Well … I have faith in you. We all have to learn our lessons, or so my mom is always telling me," this earned a smile from Grace, "so you'll learn yours in your way and then go on with life. You'll be a better person for it!"

Grace looked at Jennifer and then started laughing, "You sound like an after school special!"

"Yeah, I know, but I wasn't sure what else to say," Jennifer was laughing too. "Seriously, you are a good person. If you weren't, why would you care if you were doing mean things?"

Grace hadn't thought of that, "Okay, I'll buy that I'm on the right track at least."

"Good, then I haven't failed completely in my pep talk!" the girls heard two horns behind them and knew it was time to go, "Grace, just trust in God. You can't go wrong if you're doing what God wants you to do."

"Thanks Jennifer. You're a good friend," Grace was just realizing how true that statement was.

Grace threw herself into the car beside her mother. "Have you ever wondered if the hospital switched babies on you, and I really belong to someone else?"

Bev gave Grace a huge smile, "Every day!"

They laughed all the way home.

Grace felt better by the time she got home. She promptly went up to her room to her seat by the window. She was beginning to wonder if she was going to wear out the cushion on her chair.

Once again staring at nothing, Grace let her mind wander. The first thing she thought about was how much fun she had with Jennifer that weekend. She was a great person, why did Grace feel like she shouldn't be seen with her? Grace couldn't understand her own actions.

Jennifer had said to just trust in God. How did one do that? Grace had been feeling God moving in her life. She knew each time she was successful with a weekly challenge she felt closer to God. The good feelings she had been having were great, and she had also been catching herself praying more and feeling more at peace. She had often surprised herself in the past few weeks by saying silent prayers for help and guidance. That had to mean something didn't it? Grace felt like something big was going to happen in her life. She just had to let it happen. Would she have the courage to do that? She looked up into the heavens and felt hopeful.

nine

GRACE FELT NER-vous at school on Monday. She didn't know if she actually had an argument with Hope last week or not when she had stood up for Jennifer. She had no idea how everyone was going to treat her today. She tried to say a prayer but the words wouldn't come. She walked into school feeling like she was entering a world of unknowns.

She didn't see Christina and Hope before first hour. Grace felt she had been given a reprieve, no matter how short it might be. She made it through the morning feeling pretty good until the bell rang signaling lunch. Then Grace felt her stomach knot up and her mouth go dry. The unknown was getting to her.

She had actually remembered her lunch today, unusual for Grace on a Monday, so she headed straight to the table. She wasn't hurrying. In fact she was taking almost as long as it would have taken to stand in line for a tray. When she finally shuffled toward the table, she was running seriously low on courage. As she looked up at the table, she suddenly stopped in her tracks. She wasn't sure what to do next.

Her usual spot had been taken. Yvette was sitting in her seat. Okay, thought Grace, she could take this punishment. She looked around the table. That's when her hands really started to shake. There were no open seats anywhere around Hope's table.

Okay, Grace thought again, I'll sit at the second table. "The group" was always too big to fit around one table and had two staked out that they used every day. She turned to her right and started to walk in that direction. That's when she realized with a glance that there were no open seats at that table either.

Grace could barely breathe now. She felt cold, yet she could feel the sweat trickling down her back. How long could she stand here without moving before someone noticed? How long before someone started pointing at her and laughing? She hoped she wouldn't start crying to top off her mortification.

Okay, she had been thinking about how she wasn't happy being a part of "the group", but she hadn't figured out what she was going to do about it. Well, it was time to figure it out. She had to get her feet to move. Standing there like a mute statue was only going to make her look more like a fool.

Grace finally regained enough muscle control to turn and take a few steps. That's when she faced the next question. Where was she going? She had sat in the same place all year. Who was she supposed to turn to now?

She did a quick glance around the room, trying not to be too obvious about her predicament. She caught sight of a couple of girls she said hi to in the hallway on a regular basis. She started toward them, trying to keep a normal pace. When she saw an open seat across the table from them she could have cried with relief.

"Hi you guys! Mind if I join you?" Grace tried to sound casual and cheery when she was really on the verge of tears.

"Umm, sure, Grace. Have a seat," Carrie sounded nice but a bit confused.

"Great!" Grace sat down feeling like she'd been delivered from a fate worse than death.

Lunch went fairly well. Grace tried to be nice and friendly. The girls she was sitting with were friendly but obviously wondering what was going on. She couldn't believe this was happening to her. She ate her lunch and smiled and then said bye quickly when the bell finally rang. It had to be the longest lunch break Grace could remember.

She rushed to band looking forward to some time with a real friend. She and Jennifer had a fun hour whispering and making music, just like usual. She caught herself saying a prayer of thanks as she left the band room. She was a little stunned she was saying thank you on a day like this, but it was how she was feeling.

Grace wondered what was going to happen after sixth hour. She met Christina at their locker every day at that time. Their encounters never consisted of more than the exchange of a few words, but they were usually fairly pleasant. It was the only time they really ever spoke without someone else being around. She didn't know how Christina might treat her today. She took a deep breath and went about her business of exchanging books and folders. Christina never showed up. Grace decided she must have taken extra books with her after lunch.

"Well, I guess I'm being taught a lesson today," Grace mumbled to herself. She was looking forward to going home today, even more than usual.

Back at home, Grace put down her backpack and took a moment to look around. This was her home. She was safe here. Her family could be a pain in the neck at times, but she was loved and accepted. She grinned as she thought about how lucky she really was.

Bev saw Grace come in and was about to call out a greeting when she saw Grace stop in the doorway. She watched her look around and then smile. Bev felt her heart warm and her eyes begin to swim. She could tell from a glance that something had happened at school today, but she could also tell that Grace knew home was a haven. Bev was grateful for that. Providing a warm, secure place for her children was very important to her.

It was a mystery to Grace that she was able to smile at all. After what had happened today, she would have expected to be a complete wreck. As she thought about how she had felt in the cafeteria, she knew she had not enjoyed the day, but she wasn't as crushed by the lunchtime shunning as she would have expected to be. This was something else to think about. She hoped once again that her brain wouldn't explode.

Grace entered school the next day feeling pretty much like she had the day before. She still didn't know what was going to happen as she walked into the building. She felt a bit better prepared today, but she could still feel the butterflies running into each other in her stomach.

Once again, she did not see any of "the group" before school started. That meant she was going to have to go to lunch not knowing what was going on yet again. When the bell rang, Grace took a deep breath, grabbed her lunch, and walked slowly into the unknown.

She could feel her hands trembling before she even got to the cafeteria door. She stepped into the large room feeling like everyone was staring at her. She shook her head. She was making herself out to be more important to everyone than she really was. She figured the truth of the matter was that very few people even realized she was in the room. She wasn't sure which scenario she liked least.

Grace made her way slowly toward "the group". She could see before she got too close that once again there were no open seats. She could feel the cold sweat again and a sudden weakness in her legs. She silently prayed for help over and over as she looked around for a place of refuge.

She found a seat this time with a small group of girls who played flute in the band. They seemed a little surprised, just like the girls yesterday, when she asked to join them, but no one seemed upset about her sitting down. Grace slumped into a seat. She wasn't sure how long she could do this.

AFTER WHAT HAPPENED THE PAST TWO DAYS, WHEN Grace entered the cafeteria on Wednesday she was already sweating. She tried to look like it was a normal day as she sauntered in to see what was going to happen today. She could see at a glance that her seat was left open today. Apparently her punishment was over. With a sigh of relief, she started to walk toward her seat, and then she stopped.

What was she doing now? She should be running to sit down. She should be feeling grateful her friends weren't mad at her anymore—shouldn't she? That was, in fact, not how she was feeling. She was feeling like she could not sit in that seat again. She could not go back to forced smiling and pretending to be someone whom she was not. She could not even decide at that moment if she would actually call the girls in "the group" her friends.

Grace forced herself to turn around. Now that she had actually acknowledged her feelings, she could not let herself lose courage. She had to do what she knew was right for her. She really wanted to turn around and just take her seat and act like it was any other normal day. She figured the rest of the girls would just pretend nothing had happened the past two days. Why couldn't she just do that too? She desperately wanted to take the easy way out, but she could not allow herself to do that. She had to do this. She had to change some things, and this was where she was going to start, even if she fainted in the process.

"Please give me courage," she begged of God as she felt herself getting light-headed. She began to look around for a place to sit.

She did find another place to sit that day. She had had

to walk almost all the way around the cafeteria. Her stomach was hurting so badly by the time she found a seat with a couple of girls from her Spanish class, that she could barely eat. She barely spoke or was spoken to during lunch, but she was intensely grateful not to be sitting alone. She smiled at the girls as the bell rang and then made a break for the band room.

The rest of the week was very much the same. She sat with the flute players again on Thursday and found a new group to invade on Friday. Grace was truly exhausted when she got home Friday afternoon. She wasn't sure she could survive this much longer. She had no idea doing the right thing could be so hard.

Grace made her way into the kitchen as soon as she got home. As she stared into the refrigerator, she thought about how simple things had seemed last year. Now this year, she was trying to deal with the change in her best friend and the change in her feeling toward faith, all while trying to keep up with her schoolwork. She was happy with her blossoming faith. It made her feel like she was doing the right thing. She had even begun to read a few verses from her Bible before she went to bed each night. But the change in her best friend was something she was having trouble getting used to.

Grace believed that if she had been shunned in the cafeteria at the beginning of the year she would have been devastated. She may have even tried not to go back to school the next day, although she was sure she wouldn't have gotten away with that. She was proud she had been able to stand on her own this week. She hadn't run screaming to the bathroom or tried to hide out from everyone. She wasn't sure how all the people she had been sitting with felt, but she was happy with how she had handled things.

"Are you trying to refrigerate the whole house Gracie?" Bev walked in from the hallway. "Sorry, Grace."

"Oh, guess I got lost in my thoughts," Grace said as she closed the refrigerator door, "And you know, I don't mind Gracie, at least not from you. It was Christina who said it sounded too babyish for an eighth grader. I never really cared."

Bev was surprised, "Ok, well, I won't worry so much when I slip up from now on."

"Good," Grace bounded up the stairs with her mom staring after her wondering who had come home that day.

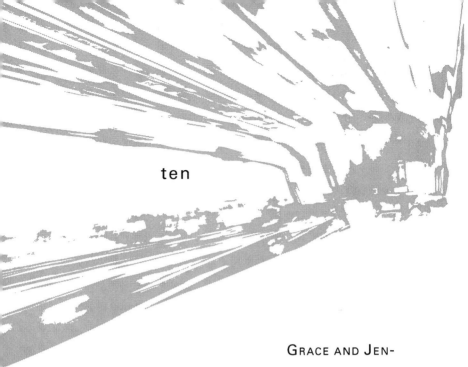

ten

GRACE AND JEN-
nifer rented movies on Saturday and took
them to Grace's house. They had a great
time laughing, crying, and talking. By the
time they'd worked their way through
their stack of movies, it was getting late.
After talking to Bev, they called Jennifer's
parents, who agreed that Jennifer could
spend the night. They would pick her up
at church the next morning.

In church the next morning, the girls
sat together trying not to yawn too often.
They had a great night but hadn't slept
much. They had discussed everything

they could think of, but Grace had not brought up her lunch room experience. She wasn't sure why, but she didn't feel like talking about it yet. She thought that maybe she needed to figure out some stuff before she could share it.

After church, Grace went home and headed to bed. She knew she better take a nap if she was going to make it through bowling with the youth group later that evening. She was looking forward to seeing how that was going to work out. She wasn't a big bowler, but she knew she and Jennifer would have fun. She hadn't really spent much time with any of the other youth outside of the meetings, so she wondered how they would all get along. She was a little nervous, but mostly she was excited.

It turned out that Grace had a fantastic time that night. She learned she was a horrible bowler, with her high score barely breaking eighty, but that didn't seem to matter. All of the youth had fun together. They did seem to break into groups according to age, but no one was left out. They all had some good laughs.

Mr. Fuller tried to get their attention, "Hey, everyone! Before you go, I want to remind you to continue your challenge this week. Continue working to do the right thing, even when it is very difficult. Put your faith and hope in God because all other hope is false hope! Remember God is always with you—even when you're at the bowling alley!"

Everyone cheered and then headed out to their cars or to meet their parents. Grace truly had a great time, but it was a relief to get home to the relative quiet. With Ryan around, things were never completely peaceful, but at least it was a few steps down from the chaos of the bowling alley.

Grace flopped down by her window to let her brain have some time to mull over the events of the past week. She had already decided she could not go back to the way things had been. Even though her seat had been left open for her after the two days of punishment, she knew it would not last forever. Eventually, if she didn't go back to sitting there, the seat would go to someone else. It was amazing to Grace that the thought of this didn't upset her.

The thought of wandering around the cafeteria looking for someone to sit with did upset her. She felt like she had gotten lucky last week when she found a place for herself each day. How long would that luck last? How long could she expect these other people to keep letting her butt into their groups? She hadn't really felt a part of any of the groups she sat with. They were all polite to her, but they didn't seem exactly thrilled to have her with them. She shook her head as she felt it starting to hurt.

Another strange thing she dealt with last week was Christina. After Monday and Tuesday, she came back to the locker after sixth hour. She talked to Grace just as she had before, as if nothing had changed.

"Maybe she didn't notice I wasn't at the table," Grace thought smugly. But she knew that wasn't true. After the intentional shut out at the beginning of the week, she was sure "the group" had been curious to see her reaction to being allowed back into the fold. She wondered if they were surprised when she didn't run back to the table.

She was surprised. She hadn't known she had that much courage. She knew maybe it shouldn't be that big of a deal to not know where you were going to sit or who you were going to sit with at lunch, but it was. She was not looking forward to the fear and uncertainty she would face again tomorrow. She bowed her head and said a prayer asking for the strength and courage to continue doing what she knew was the right thing for her. She was finished with her false hope. She was placing her faith in God.

Grace had to chase down the bus the next morning, but she did make it to school. She was wishing for a calmer start to her day. She didn't need any more stress. She had the familiar feeling of butterflies fluttering around in her stomach the entire morning.

At lunchtime, Grace entered the cafeteria only after taking a deep breath. She had her lunch in her hand as she began to look for a place to sit. Luckily, the first person she saw was Jennifer. She invited Grace to join them. Grace sat down with a huge smile on her face. She knew she was going to have a great afternoon.

Later that day, Grace sat thinking in her usual spot. She didn't know why she didn't feel like she could sit with Jennifer every day. She did feel like they were good friends, and Jennifer always told Grace to join them any time, but Grace just couldn't be sure if she really meant it. She had never known Jennifer to say anything she didn't mean, and they always had a good time together. Why couldn't she just sit with them and stop her daily torture? She couldn't seem to come up with an answer, but she was determined to figure it out.

She had some help with her figuring the next day. When Grace arrived at school, she ran into Christina, literally, in the hallway as she was making her way to her locker.

"Oof, hi, Christina! Sorry about that," Grace fought to keep her balance.

"That's ok. These halls are crazy," Christina didn't seem upset.

"Yeah, I don't remember them being so bad last year." Christina smoothed her hair as she talked, "I don't think they were. I can't imagine where all these people came from."

Grace was intrigued that Christina was still talking with her, so she tried to continue the conversation, "I've heard my dad talking about how many people are moving to Patton. I never thought that would mean running over people in the halls at school!"

"I know, I've heard some …"Christina broke off suddenly, "Ya know. I've got to, uh, go to the bathroom. See you later, Grace."

Grace watched with her mouth hanging open as Christina jumped into the bathroom just on the other side of the hall from them. As she turned to go to her locker, Grace glanced back at the bathroom door just as Hope and "the group" walked past. Grace knew exactly what had happened. Christina hadn't wanted to be seen with her.

Grace could feel her blood pressure rising. How could she do that to her? They had been friends for years, and now she wasn't worthy even to talk to in the halls? Grace muttered to herself in anger as she organized her books in her locker. She could not believe Christina had done that to her.

As she slammed her locker door to head to class, a realization slammed into Grace. What Christina had done to her was almost exactly the same thing she had done to Jennifer at the mall. She hadn't wanted to be seen by "the group" then, just like Christina hadn't wanted to be seen by them today. Now what was she going to do?

At lunch Grace sat with another group of girls she knew from class. She just hadn't felt like she could impose on Jennifer and her friends. She had decided she was going to have to apologize to Jennifer before she could do anything else with her. She knew Jennifer didn't even know what she had done, but Grace knew. She knew she would only feel like she was being a true friend when she told Jennifer the truth.

Grace made her first attempt to apologize in band. She and Jennifer were talking before class as they usually did.

Grace cleared her throat and began to talk, "Uh, Jennifer I have something I need to tell you."

Jennifer smiled, "Ok, I'm all ears."

Grace had no idea how to start, "Well, I, uh, really like spending time with you. I think we have a lot of fun together."

"Oh, I agree. You are a great friend!" Jennifer said with enthusiasm.

Not too great, Grace thought. As she opened her mouth to continue, Mrs. Schwear stepped up to her podium and started class. There would be no apology during band class that day.

That evening at home, Grace called Jennifer. She was determined to apologize. Unfortunately, Jennifer wasn't home. Grace wondered where she could be. Things weren't working out as she had hoped. She wanted to get this apology over with, but no one else would cooperate.

Grace lay down on her bed and stared up at the ceiling. She was going to be the kind of friend people wanted to hang around with, not one people tried to avoid or run away from.

She was going to be honest and trustworthy. This time, she wasn't surprised as she began to pray.

"Dear Lord, I know I'm a mess. It seems I'm having lots of trouble making good decisions. The things I've been hoping for and believing I want and need really aren't so important. Please help me see what's important, Lord. Please forgive me when I do the wrong things. I'm so tired of doing the wrong thing and hurting people, or myself. I'm tired of trying to be someone that's not really me. I really want to do the right thing. Please be with me. In Jesus' name I pray, Amen."

Grace rolled over and sat up. She heard a noise in the hall. The thud was followed by a bang and then a bark. Grace smiled. Ryan had come upstairs. She decided to do her homework and then get to bed.

Grace was still determined to clear her conscience the next morning. She decided she was going to get to lunch as fast as possible and try to find Jennifer before she sat down. Maybe she could talk to her before they were sitting at a table full of people.

As the bell rang after fourth hour, Grace put her plan into action. She moved as quickly as she could and was soon standing in the cafeteria. Instead of beginning her search for a place to sit, Grace kept her eye on the door. As soon as she spotted Jennifer, she took a deep breath and hurried over.

"Hey, Jennifer!" Grace called out. Jennifer turned toward the back of the room, and Grace was afraid she was about to lose her chance again.

"Oh, hi Grace," Jennifer was all smiles as usual.

"I'm glad I caught you! I really want to talk to you about something before you sit down."

"Sure," Jennifer said as she stepped over closer to the wall to keep from getting run over by others trying to get into the room.

Grace followed Jennifer and then plunged in, "Okay, this is kind of hard for me to say. I really never wanted to hurt your feelings. I really want to be a good friend, but I have to say this before we do anything else."

As Grace paused to catch her breath, Jennifer just looked at her and said, "Whatever it is, I'm sure it will be alright. Just spit it out."

"Ok, here goes. You remember when we went to the mall a couple weeks back, after we saw the movie?" As Jennifer nodded, Grace hurried on, "Ok, well, while we were in the mall, while we were window shopping, I saw Hope and some of her friends walking toward us. I didn't know what they might say to me or to you, so I talked you into going inside the store. I know I was afraid they might say something mean. I'm so sorry. I never planned to hurt you. I'm sorry. I know it sounds like I didn't want to be seen with you. I just wanted to say I'm sorry, and I am definitely not embarrassed to be seen with you. I'll understand if you need some time to forgive me, but I am sorry."

Grace started to walk away. She knew she had talked a little fast and had repeated herself several times, but she felt good about the apology. She was just mad at herself for hurting Jennifer's feelings. She could just kick herself for doing this to such a nice person. Why couldn't she be a good friend?

"Oh, Grace! I can see your imagination is running away with you again!" Grace turned back around and almost smiled at how well Jennifer already knew her. "I'm not mad at you.

Believe it or not, I saw Hope and her friends that day at the mall. I knew you spent time with them, but, and I don't mean to sound mean, I never knew why. She just doesn't seem like, like, hmmm, like you. I guess I never could figure out what you have in common with Hope. I just figured you were you and you could pick your own friends. I didn't really want to run into Hope that day either. I didn't want her to be mean to you, so I didn't mind one bit hiding out in that store."

"So you're really not mad?" Grace was having a hard time believing what she was hearing. She had never even considered that Jennifer had seen Hope that day.

"No, I'm not mad. But I do know now you really are a great friend."

"I'm trying," Grace said softly.

"No one else I know would have bothered to apologize for something they didn't even think I knew about! Now, come on. Let's eat lunch before we run out of time."

Grace happily followed Jennifer to the table. She was so grateful things had worked out! Her prayer of thanks came straight from her heart.

GRACE WAS FEELING LIKE SHE WAS GETTING HER LIFE back on track. She was humming a tune as she walked into the house that afternoon. Her mom walked up behind her.

"Hey, you! Have a good day did ya?"

"Hey, mom! Yes, as a matter of fact I did have good day. I think things are beginning to get better," Grace replied.

Bev could barely contain her happiness, "I'm so glad to hear that!"

"Thanks for everything Mom," Grace looked her mom right in the eye as she spoke.

"Thanks for what? I can't think of anything I've done," Grace's mom said in surprise.

"Thanks for just being there. I always knew you cared. I guess, maybe, that made things a little easier. And nothing has been easy the past several weeks," Grace gave her mom a hug and ran up the stairs.

"You're welcome. I love you," Bev called after Grace as she ran to her room.

Bev stood where she was for several minutes. She didn't want to lose the warm feeling she had at that moment. To hear those words from her daughter had been a great surprise and had touched her heart deeply. She never expected anything like this to ever happen, and she was determined to never forget it or take it for granted. Maybe she wasn't as terrible a mother as she had always thought! She felt a tear roll down her cheek just as the back door flew open, and Ryan and Avis came flying into the room in one big tumbled mess.

"Hey, Mom! Something wrong?" Ryan asked in a loud voice as he stumbled into the room.

Bev looked at him and smiled, "Nothing whatsoever!"

"Good!" Ryan flew on by up the stairs with Avis at his heels. Bev headed to the kitchen laughing. Life was good.

Grace was thinking the same thing. She was feeling good about her decisions. She still couldn't believe Jennifer knew what she did at the mall when she hid them in that store. She wondered if she would have been so nice about it. Maybe she would surprise herself one day, and she would realize she really wasn't so bad after all.

The next day at lunch, Grace stood trying to decide what to do. She really wanted to find Jennifer and sit with her, but she didn't know if she should. She didn't want the other girls, like Rebecca Frankie, to get tired of her butting in on them. Finally, she started her daily walk around looking for a place to eat.

She was just about to start sweating and shaking when she looked over and saw Jennifer's table. Jennifer looked up and waved her over. Despite her earlier misgivings, Grace quickly made her way to the table and sat down.

"What took you so long?" Jennifer asked, "People kept trying to take your chair to another table."

"Oh, sorry. I promise to be quicker tomorrow!" Grace could have cried with happiness. She knew her days of wandering aimlessly around the cafeteria were finally over. She had a seat with friends who liked her even though she was being herself. No more fake smiling for her!

At lunch, Jennifer brought up doing something together on Saturday. Grace liked the thought of spending more time getting to know the other girls who sat with Jennifer at lunch. She already knew Rebecca, who seemed to have forgiven her for her past mistake. The other three girls she had been in classes with, but she had never hung out with them. Emily she had liked right away. She had a great sense of humor and appeared to be very easy going. Michelle was a bit more serious but always had a smile on her face. The other girl at the table was more mysterious to Grace. Gretchen didn't talk as much as the others, and it was hard to maintain eye contact with her. Grace decided she was nice but probably shy. Grace knew how it felt to be shy, so she was going to give Gretchen every chance she could to feel more comfortable with her.

"How about we go to the mall?" Jennifer suggested. It was a good place to go since there were lots of different things to do in one spot.

Everyone seemed to like the idea, except for Rebecca, "Oh, I don't know if I can make it on Saturday."

Jennifer tried to change her mind, "Really? That would be too bad. I have these cool coupons for buy-one-get-one free stuff at the burger place in the center of the mall. I was hoping to find someone willing to help me eat all that food!"

"Well," Rebecca said with a smile, "I'll ask my mom."

"Great!" said Jennifer and Grace at the same time. They both knew Rebecca was worried about asking her parents for money. Grace thought Jennifer was a genius and hoped she really had some coupons. Now the plans were set. She knew this trip to the mall would not be like her last trip there. All she had to do was make it to the weekend.

When Saturday finally arrived Grace was a bundle of nerves. She wasn't sure why she was so nervous, so she didn't really have an answer when her mom asked her about it.

"I don't know," Grace answered, making a conscious choice to not be irritated by her mom knowing how she was feeling, even as she was still trying to finish figuring it out. "I've been trying to figure that out. I think that, well, hmmm, maybe ... I just want everyone to have fun with me."

"I can't imagine why they wouldn't. Just be Grace," Bev replied. She wasn't sure if she should be worried or not.

"Oh, don't worry about that! I am finished being anyone else. I guess, maybe, that's why I feel like tonight is so important. If they like me, it means they really like ME. I suppose it works the other way too. If they don't like me, it means they really don't like ME," Grace knew she was rattling, but she couldn't seem to help herself.

Bev was enjoying the conversation. She tried to take advantage of any time Grace would talk, "Well, I can't think of any reason why anyone wouldn't like you. You're kind, funny, smart, beautiful …"

"Alright! Now I know you're just saying that because you're my mom and you have to," Grace was rolling her eyes.

"Never!" Bev protested.

"Always!" Grace called back laughing. "Now I have to get upstairs and find something to wear."

"Oh, I feel sorry for your clothes. Be kind and good luck!" Bev called after Grace as she ran laughing up the stairs. Bev said a quick prayer for Grace before heading off to check on Ryan outside.

Grace was glad she wasn't the first to arrive as her mom dropped her off at the mall. Through the front doors, she saw Michelle standing by the fountain where they were all supposed to meet. She said a quick good bye to her mom and crawled out of the car. She couldn't wait to see how the evening would go.

"Hey, Michelle!" Grace called as she neared the fountains.

"Hi, Grace! I'm glad someone else is here. It was getting a little lonely here on my own," Michelle said with her usual smile.

"Oh, I know what you mean," Grace said with feeling.

It only took about ten minutes for all of the girls, including Rebecca, to arrive. They set out together to walk around and decide what they wanted to do. After a while, they decided to go into one of the more trendy stores and try on some clothes.

They picked out outfits for each other and the person whose turn it was had to try on whatever was picked out for them. Grace's sides started hurting from laughing so much. She ended up having to try on some low cut "skinny" jeans and a fuchsia tank with a little flimsy shrug. Then Emily found a pair of flip-flops with three-inch heels for her to wear with the outfit.

"I can't believe I'm doing this," Grace mumbled as she entered the dressing room with her ensemble.

"Ahh, you'll look great," Jennifer said, and then she burst out laughing.

"Thanks, I feel so much better," Grace stuck her tongue out at her as she pulled the curtain closed.

She had to struggle a bit to get the jeans on, but she was pleasantly surprised that they weren't as uncomfortable as she had expected. The tank was awful. The armholes were too big and it was way too tight. She was very glad Gretchen had taken pity on her and picked out the little shrug to wear over it or she wouldn't have been able to leave the dressing room. As she sat down to put on the shoes she discovered why she would never buy jeans like that.

"Whoa, these jeans weren't made for sitting!" she called to her friends on the other side of the curtain.

"Got a little plumber action going on in there?" Grace was surprised to hear Rebecca's voice.

"More than a little!" Grace said with a laugh. She could here the others giggling.

"Come on out here!" Jennifer called.

"Alright, you asked for it!" Grace stepped out. She wobbled dangerously in the heels. "I hope I don't break my ankles. I can't believe I'm coming out here looking like this!"

"Oh, Grace!" All five of the other girls seemed to say it in unison, "I don't really think that's your style!"

"Let me tell you—it's not! I'm quite uncomfortable, and I couldn't possibly sit down in public without getting arrested!" Grace was laughing with the rest of them.

They each took a turn in the dressing room. They were having a great time. It was when Jennifer stepped out wearing a bright purple mini skirt over black leggings with a neon blue top that tied in the front with gold, sparkling four-inch wedge shoes that Grace looked up and saw Hope and "the group". "The group" was staring at them like they were from outer space. Grace was speechless for a moment. She felt herself flashback to the last time she had been at the mall. Jennifer looked at her and winked.

"Hi, Hope. Do you think I should buy this outfit?" Jennifer was laughing as she asked the question.

Now it was Hope's turn to be speechless. She just stared without saying anything. A rare thing as Grace remembered.

"We're just having some fun," Jennifer went on, "Would you like to join us?"

"I should think not," Hope said as she turned around, tossing her hair in that way that still fascinated Grace.

"Okay, we'll see you later then," Jennifer said cheerily as "the group" made a quick exit.

Grace stared at Jennifer, "Wow, you're good!"

"What do you mean?" Jennifer asked with a mischievous look.

"You were nice, but came off like the winner in a fight," Grace said with appreciation.

"I never want to be mean. Sometimes you can kill someone with kindness, so to speak," Jennifer turned to go change her clothes.

"I think you were great. Do you think I could ever learn to flip my hair like she does?" Everyone laughed at Grace's question, including Grace.

After Jennifer got back into her clothes, the girls set off to find some food. As it turned out, Jennifer really did have some coupons for the burger place. They had a great time pigging out on burgers, fries, shakes, and even an order of onion rings.

"This is almost gross," said Emily as she woofed down another fry.

"Yep," said Gretchen, "but it sure is good."

The girls were laughing again as Hope and her group walked by. Grace saw Christina walking beside Hope. She smiled and waved to her and was pleasantly surprised when Christina waved back. Maybe all was not lost with Christina after all. She would just have to wait and see what God had in store for them next.

At home that night, Grace was practically bubbling with happiness. She was actually glad to see her mom reading in the living room. She thought she might explode if she didn't talk to someone. She ran in and plopped down beside her mom. Bev looked over her book at her.

"Oh, I'm sorry, Gracie. It appears you didn't have any fun tonight," Bev failed in her attempt to keep a straight face.

"Yep, it was awful–awful fun! It was so great! I think all of us had fun, and everyone actually seemed glad I was there!" Grace could barely sit still as she talked.

"I'm so glad to hear that! I have to admit though, I'm not terribly surprised," Bev said.

"Well, I wasn't terribly surprised I had a good time either," Grace said mimicking the way her mom had said "terribly surprised". "What did surprise me was how much of a good time we had! I mean, we really had fun!"

"You didn't do anything illegal did you?" Bev tried to look concerned.

"Get real, of course not!" Grace proceeded to tell her mom about how they tried on clothes and then went and ate until they all thought they were going to be sick.

Grace and her mom had a good laugh. Bev was counting her blessings that her daughter would talk with her like this, while Grace was counting her blessings that her mom would laugh with her like this. They both felt like they were finding their way.

Grace looked over at her mom and yawned, "Well, I'm off to bed."

"Good night then," Bev said. She tried to swallow the lump in her throat that formed as Grace bent over and kissed her good night. She could barely get out a "see you in the morning."

Grace took the stairs two at a time and quickly got ready for bed. Then she walked over and sat by her window. She was tired but her mind needed a few minutes to sort through the evening and calm down before she could get to sleep.

Downstairs, Bev walked around turning out lights and locking doors. Her mind, too, was buzzing with activity. She paused at the kitchen window. She just looked out for a few minutes.

Unknown to the other, as they both stared unseeing out the window, they both thought at the same moment, "Thank you God for the blessings in my life. Please be with me as I face whatever comes next. Amen."